Published by Kansas City Star Books
1729 Grand Boulevard
Kansas City, MO 64108

First Edition
ISBN 978-1-933466-76-7

Edited by Monroe Dodd
Book design by Jean D. Dodd

Printed in the United States of America
by Walsworth Publishing Co., Inc.
Marceline, Mo.

Based on articles written by J. Brady
McCollough of *The Kansas City Star*, and
on columns by Joe Posnanski and Jason
Whitlock of *The Star*. Other members of
The Star's staff contributed articles.
Photographs by Rich Sugg, with contri-
butions by Shane Keyser and other staff
members of *The Star* and by Jeff Tuttle of
The Wichita Eagle.
Photographs by the Associated Press on
pages 18, 19, 21,24, 27, 28, 30, 44, 45,
50, 51, 57 and 64.

UNSTOPPABLE

The Kansas Jayhawks' Journey to the NCAA Title

J. Brady McCollough   Joe Posnanski   Jason Whitlock
and the staff of *The Kansas City Star*

 KANSAS CITY STAR BOOKS

THE COACH

"Do it this way and we will win"

To understand how much the basketball season and the NCAA tournament mean to Kansas coach Bill Self, you first have to understand this: Every single day, in one way or another, he tells his players that they are unstoppable.

Every day. Sometimes he yells it during practice. Sometimes he tells them in the locker room before the game. Sometimes he announces it on a bus ride. Sometimes he just pulls a player aside, wraps an arm around the player's shoulder, whispers it in his ear. Always, though, the message remains.

You cannot be stopped. You cannot be blocked out. You cannot be screened. You are too strong. You are too tough. You are too fast. You have come too far. You have worked too hard. You have sacrificed too much.

You are unstoppable!

Every day for 15 years, in one way or another, this has been what he has told his college basketball players. Self does not claim to be a strategic genius. He has had great success in recent years recruiting talented players, but that's not what defines him. He has won 349 games, and he's only 45 years old, and he's coached Kansas to a national championship.

Yet the thing that Bill Self believes most about himself is that – through hard work, through intense teaching, through blunt honesty and a little bullying and the lessons of hard experience and a lot of charm – he can convince a bunch of college kids that no team in America can stop them. Unstoppable! That's the word. That's his word.

And yet ... all along the way, they had been stopped. Self had been stopped. Five times, at three different schools, Bill Self had coached his players to the Elite Eight – to the shadow of college basketball's nirvana, the Final Four. The first four times his teams lost. Until this season, among active coaches he had the most NCAA Tournament victories without a Final Four appearance.

2008 marked the fifth chance. He made it to the Final Four and beyond.

"There is never any doubt with coach Self," Kansas guard Brandon Rush says. "He makes it very clear: 'Do it this way and we will stop them. Do it this way and we will score. Do it this way and we will win.'"

Joe Posnanski

THE TEAM

The 2007-08 season truly began May 24, 2007, when Brandon Rush tore his right anterior cruciate ligament in a pickup game at home in Kansas City while preparing for the NBA's pre-draft camp in Orlando, Fla. If not for the injury, Rush said, he would not have returned to KU.

Self's heart went out to Rush, but KU's coach knew that his team just got a lot better.

When "Late Night at the Phog" rolled around in October, there was Rush after four months of rehab, wearing a suit and dancing on that right knee. It was the most highly-scrutinized dance number in "Late Night" history, to be sure.

"Late Night" also introduced KU's five-man senior class. The year before, when KU lost in the Elite Eight to UCLA, there were no seniors. But Russell Robinson, Darnell Jackson and Sasha Kaun were a part of Self's first recruiting class, and they stuck it out until the end.

Kansas bounded out to a 20-0 record. There was already of an undefeated regular season for the Jayhawks. But then KU lost to Kansas State on Jan. 30 and twice more on the road in February. The Jayhawks were no longer in the driver's seat for a Big 12 regular-season title and a No. 1 seed in the NCAA Tournament.

That's when the senior Jayhawks called a players-only meeting on Feb. 24, the day after the loss to Oklahoma State. The players aired out their frustrations over chicken wings and sandwiches. They never lost again.

When the NCAA Tournament brackets came out, it felt like 1988 all over again, the year KU won its last national championship. The reminders were there, staring Kansas in the face – games in Nebraska and then in Michigan. It had to be their year.

It was. On the night of April 7, the seniors and the underclassmen hugged and held the NCAA trophy in San Antonio.

J. Brady McCollough

ROSTER

No.	Name	Yr.	Pos.	Ht.	Wt.	Hometown
00	Darrell Arthur	So	Forward	6-9	225	Dallas, Texas
2	Conner Teahan	Fr	Guard	6-5	205	Leawood, Kan.
3	Russell Robinson	Sr	Guard	6-1	205	New York, N.Y.
4	Sherron Collins	So	Guard	5-11	205	Chicago, Ill.
5	Rodrick Stewart	Sr	Guard	6-4	200	Seattle, Wash.
10	Jeremy Case	Sr	Guard	6-1	190	McAlester, Okla.
11	Brennan Bechard	Jr	Guard	6-0	185	Lawrence, Kan.
12	Brady Morningstar	So	Guard	6-3	187	Lawrence, Kan.
14	Tyrel Reed	Fr	Guard	6-3	185	Burlington, Kan.
15	Mario Chalmers	Jr	Guard	6-1	190	Anchorage, Alaska
22	Chase Buford	Fr	Guard	6-3	200	San Antonio, Texas
24	Sasha Kaun	Sr	Center	6-11	250	Melbourne, Fla.
25	Brandon Rush	Jr	Guard	6-6	210	Kansas City, Mo.
32	Darnell Jackson	Sr	Forward	6-8	250	Oklahoma City, Okla.
40	Brad Witherspoon	Sr	Guard	6-1	190	Humboldt, Kan.
45	Cole Aldrich	Fr	Center	6-11	240	Bloomington, Minn.
54	Matt Kleinmann	Jr	Center	6-10	250	Overland Park, Kan.

Coaches

Bill Self - Head Coach
Danny Manning - Assistant Coach
Joe Dooley - Assistant Coach
Kurtis Townsend - Assistant Coach
Brett Ballard - Administrative Assistant/Video Coordinator
Ronnie Chalmers - Director of Basketball Operations

After their victory in the NCAA final game, the Jayhawks watched the annual tournament highlight video.

The 1988 Jayhawks with their NCAA trophy, above. At the beginning of the tournament, sixth-seeded KU seemed an unlikely candidate for the crown.
Right: One KU fan wore his 1988 champion-ship souvenir T-shirt to San Antonio for the 2008 game.

THE LAST TIME

At the start of the 1988 tournament, KU's prospects seemed meager. Then Danny and the Miracles went to work.

Kansas trainer Mark Cairns and Kevin Pritchard went to the Devaney Center in Lincoln, Neb., early on the day of KU's first-round NCAA tournament game against Xavier in March 1988. Pritchard, the team's point guard, had sprained his knee in the first round of the Big Eight tournament.

The Jayhawks were a No. 6 seed in the NCAA. With a roster reduced by academic ineligibility, injury and poor attitude to nine basketball players and two players recruited from the football team, KU needed every player it had.

Cairns and Pritchard went through a shootaround to test his knee, and Cairns worried that Pritchard wouldn't be himself. Then Pritchard took the opening tip down the floor and dunked. So much for concern. That evening, the Jayhawks ran Xavier out of the building, 85-72.

Suddenly, things began to shape up nicely for KU. No. 3 seed North Carolina State, the Jayhawks' likely opponent, was upset by No. 14 seed Murray State. The Racers were hungry for more, played with KU's emotions all game long, and came within three points of another upset, but KU won, 61-58. Danny Manning hit two clutch free throws down the stretch to clinch it.

"One shot against Murray State," Pritchard says, "and we're out of it."

Teammate Scooter Barry says: "That was the heartbeat game, the one that really got me nervous."

The Jayhawks' hearts were beating all right. They left Lincoln with a feeling of, "Well, why the hell not?" If only their fans had felt the same way. As KU's team bus pulled up at Allen Fieldhouse late that night, nobody was waiting to congratulate them.

On to the Midwest Regional in Pontiac, Mich. Even KU couldn't deny its good fortune in facing No. 7 seed Vanderbilt, which knocked off No. 2 seed Pittsburgh in the second round.

The Jayhawks certainly didn't apologize when Manning poured in 38 points in a 77-64 victory over the Commodores in the Sweet 16. And the Jayhawks didn't apologize when No. 4 seed K-State beat No. 1 seed Purdue the same day.

Suddenly, the only thing standing in the way of the Jayhawks and the Final Four, which happened that year to be in Kansas City, was rival K-State. The Wildcats had beaten KU in two of three contests already that season.

Danny Manning and Chris Piper celebrated the 1988 championship victory at Kemper Arena.

In Pontiac, however, KU settled the score with an all-too-easy 71-58 win over the Wildcats.

On Saturday night, in the semifinals at Kemper Arena, Kansas put aside any doubts about whether it could hang with the Duke Blue Devils when it jumped out to a 14-0 lead, which would balloon to 24-6. Manning finished with 25 points, 10 rebounds, four steals and six blocked shots as KU advanced 66-59 to face Oklahoma, which beat Arizona in the other semifinal game.

For three weeks, the Jayhawks had lived in the moment. While they stayed grounded, their coach agonized over everything. Coach Larry Brown, known for his superstitions, had actually flown in the same bus driver from KU's Sweet 16 and Elite Eight victories in Detroit to drive the bus in Kansas City.

Detail-minded? Yes.

Crazy? Perhaps.

But it would take something crazy for the Jayhawks to beat Billy Tubbs' big-talking Oklahoma Sooners. At least, it seemed that way.

"Oklahoma was cocky, they were flamboyant," Barry says. "We were kind of a testament to Larry Brown. We were more

controlled and dignified. It was kind of like the rebels against the clean-cut guys."

KU legend Wilt Chamberlain picked the Sooners in that morning's USA Today. CBS commentator Billy Packer, who announced the game, was convinced that KU could not run with the Sooners.

Fittingly, the Jayhawks decided that was exactly what they'd do. Punch the Sooners in the mouth. Show that they weren't intimidated like everyone else. The Jayhawks turned the ball over often, but it didn't matter because they made 17 of their first 20 shots.

KU went to the half tied 50-50. While the Sooners used only six players, Brown subbed more than he had all season.

"He was shuffling guys in and out like a Vegas card dealer," Barry says.

Barry was on the floor at the end of the game. Once a walk-on with seemingly little potential, he had to make a free throw to boost KU's lead to 79-77 with 16 seconds left. Manning would ice the game with four freebies, and the Jayhawks won 83-79. The players all ran to Manning, who finished with 31 points and 18 rebounds.

In the afterglow, Alvin Gentry, an assistant, looked at Brown.

"We won the national championship with Scooter Barry," Gentry said.

It wasn't a slam at Barry. It was reality. The Jayhawks had made history, becoming the first team to win a title with as many as 11 losses.

Soon, though, the good times would end. Manning, of course, was gone, graduated, headed to the NBA. In June, Brown decided to join him, leaving with his entire staff for the San Antonio Spurs head coaching job. The program hired Roy Williams, a young buck with no college head coaching experience.

In November, news broke that the NCAA was putting the program on probation for improper benefits given to a potential transfer student, a player named Vincent Askew. The NCAA discovered that KU, under Brown's direction in 1986, had paid for Askew's flights to and from Kansas, among other things.

Brown was long gone, but that was irrelevant to the NCAA infractions committee, which handed KU a 1989 postseason ban. The Jayhawks made a different kind of history, becoming the first national champions that couldn't defend their title.

J. Brady McCollough

Non-conference

WARMING UP

Before the games started counting, the Jayhawks took on a couple of intrastate foes in Allen Fieldhouse. The contests were called exhibitions, and each was an exhibition of Kansas' scoring prowess.

Nov. 1, 2007

Pittsburg State Gorillas

Allen Fieldhouse

Points, yes, but energy?

Sophomore guard Sherron Collins led the Jayhawks against the Gorillas from Pittsburg, Kan., with 18 points, half from three-point baskets. Collins also had five assists and four steals. Junior guard Mario Chalmers added 14 points, all in the first half, and connected on four of five attempts from beyond the arc. The Jayhawks, however, were outrebounded by the Gorillas 36-33 and after the game Coach Bill Self lamented his team's lack of energy.

The next day, sophomore guard Brady Morningstar – buried on the KU bench behind Russell Robinson, Mario Chalmers, Sherron Collins, Brandon Rush and Rodrick Stewart – told Self he would take a redshirt and sit out the 2007-2008 season.

Final:

Kansas **94**
Pittsburg State 59

Sherron Collins sailed past Pittsburg State's Justin McCoy for a shot in the first half.

Facing page: Lined up for a pre-season team portrait, Collins showed walk-on Brennan Bechard his biceps.

As Fort Hays State's Ryan Herrman watched, Darrell Arthur took a pass from Russell Robinson for a behind-the-head dunk.

Nov. 6, 2007

Fort Hays State Tigers

Allen Fieldhouse

The long lob

In KU's second exhibition, sophomore forward Darrell Arthur opened each half with an alley-oop dunk, and scored the last of his 20 points with a behind-the-back alley-oop slam. He also got eight rebounds. It was easy to lob the ball to Arthur against the Tigers, an NCAA Division II school from Hays, Kan. Fort Hays featured only one player taller than 6 feet 6.

"He's got a great inside game," senior guard Russell Robinson said of Arthur. "We're going to play through him a lot."

The Jayhawks held a 47-22 advantage in rebounds. Kansas' pressure defense overwhelmed Fort Hays from the opening tip, holding the Tigers scoreless for the first five minutes.

Final:

Kansas **93**
Fort Hays State........................56

THE GAMES BEGIN

Nov. 9, 2007

Louisiana-Monroe Warhawks

Allen Fieldhouse

Bodying up to the scoreboard

Senior Darnell Jackson talks like an inside banger and looks like an inside banger, but on this night he showed a larger dimension, scoring a career-high 21 points in Kansas' victory over the Louisiana-Monroe Warhawks. Jackson, who averaged 4.7 points per game his first three seasons, worked in the offseason to make himself more of a part of KU's offense.

"Yeah, I had 21 points, but it's no big deal," Jackson said. "My job isn't to score. My job is to do the dirty work."

Jackson, an Oklahoma City native, played 7 minutes a game his freshman year and just more than 15 minutes a game the next two years as he slowly developed into a dependable inside presence for the Jayhawks. With starting center Sasha Kaun struggling offensively in the first games of the season, Jackson's scoring was a welcome addition to the dirty work he normally performs. Most of his points came near the rim against a small Louisiana-Monroe lineup, but he swished a 17-foot jump shot and finished a hanging layup for a three-point play. Jackson made all five of his free-throw attempts.

"He's a very good perimeter face-up shooter," Self said.

KU, ranked fourth in the country in the polls, had an easy time scoring against the Warhawks; sophomore guard Sherron Collins led all scorers with 22 points. Yet the Jayhawks struggled to slow down their guards. Louisiana-Monroe shot 51 percent, becoming just the third team in the last 75 games to shoot more than 50 percent against KU.

"To get 78 hung on you in your own building …," Self grumbled. "I thought in all honesty our guards didn't guard their guards very well at all tonight."

The Jayhawks had 48 points from their bench – led by Jackson's 21, freshman Tyrel Reed's 11 and freshman Cole Aldrich's six.

The game's leading scorer, Sherron Collins, drove on Jonas Brown of Louisiana-Monroe.

Final score:

Kansas **107**

Louisiana-Monroe 78

Nov. 11, 2007

University of Missouri-Kansas City Kangaroos

Allen Fieldhouse

A little sweat

KU came away with a fairly easy victory but the scrappy Kangaroos from UMKC made them feel just a tad uncomfortable.

"They played with as much energy as we did," guard Russell Robinson said. "They came out intense and we had to match it."

Whenever UMKC made a small dent in Kansas' double-digit lead in the second half, the Jayhawks turned up their defense. When KU extended its lead to 62-48 on a three-pointer by Robinson with just more than 9 minutes left, an undaunted UMKC team fought back.

"I thought truthfully, we outhustled them tonight," UMKC coach Matt Brown said. "I think in terms of effort we were right there with them."

A soft runner in the lane by senior Jeremiah Hartsock pulled UMKC within 10 at 62-52. But the Jayhawks quickly answered with five straight points, ending any chance UMKC had of shocking the state of Kansas.

"It was good for us to sweat and to play under some duress," coach Bill Self said.

KU guard Mario Chalmers scored 23 points, most of his career. Darrell Arthur was solid inside, scoring 13 points and pulling down 10 rebounds.

Final score

Kansas **85**

UMKC 62

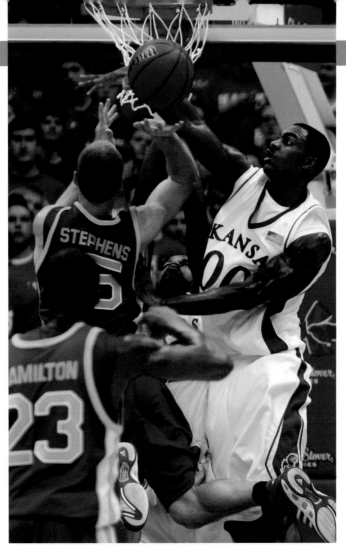

Left: Darrell Arthur smacked down a shot by UMKC's Brent Stephens in the first half.
Below: Mario Chalmers, leading scorer in the game, slipped past Reggie Hamilton of UMKC on his way to the basket.

Nov. 15, 2007

Washburn Ichabods
Allen Fieldhouse

Trading places

One Jayhawk was down, but another came back.

Guard Sherron Collins, victim of a sprained left ankle in KU's victory over UMKC four days beforehand, was found to have a stress fracture in his left foot. The result was surgery that kept him out of this game and was expected to keep him out for weeks.

On the other hand, a few minutes into the game against the Ichabods, Brandon Rush jogged casually to the scorer's table and sat there in a catcher's stance. With 16:17 left in the first half, he entered the game, his first appearance in six months. A massive brace surrounding his right knee, he was greeted by a raucous standing ovation from the 16,300 fans. Rush contributed to a KU victory.

Through 24 weeks of grueling rehabilitation from surgery on his torn right anterior cruciate ligament, Rush had beaten deadlines for his recovery. Although he expected to return on Dec. 1, KU's doctors gave him the go-ahead for 10 to 15 minutes of action this night.

Collins had been KU's leading scorer after two games, but Rush had led the team in scoring the year before. He played 12 minutes in the first half, scoring seven points on three-of-five shooting and adding three rebounds and two assists. He played so much in the first half that KU coach Bill Self had no choice but to hold him out for the entire second half. Rush settled for sideline banter with the recuperating Collins.

KU looked as if it missed Collins during the first half, limping out to a 22-16 lead with 6:11 left. The Jayhawks, as a group, had not been happy with their defense.

"We're letting people get in their comfort zone," said Rush, who acknowledged his defense wasn't where it needed to be either. "I don't think we're pressuring a lot."

Final score

Kansas....................................**92**

Washburn 60

Rodrick Stewart, above, started the game for the Jayhawks and put heavy pressure on Washburn's James Williams. Right: Brandon Rush came back from knee surgery, playing a few minutes in the first half and then joining injured teammate Sherron Collins on the bench in the second half.

Sasha Kaun put pressure on Northern Arizona's Cameron Jones.

Nov. 21, 2007

Northern Arizona Lumberjacks *Allen Fieldhouse*

The heat turned up

Before the season began, the Kansas Jayhawks talked often about how hungry they were. Against Northern Arizona, they finally showed it, dismantling the Lumberjacks and looking as if they had been fasting for weeks.

The Jayhawks held their opponent to 10 first-half points. They forced 15 turnovers, blocked six shots and created five steals and led 44-10 at halftime.

"I'd give it a 10," said forward Darnell Jackson of KU's first-half defense. "The intensity was going through the roof."

The Lumberjacks of the Big Sky Conference were no match.

The entire season, Coach Bill Self had been clamoring for the Jayhawks to turn up the heat on the opposition. For this game, Jackson said, Self gave the players a challenge: "Try not to let them score." So KU contested every shot from the start. On Northern Arizona's first two trips down the floor, KU center Sasha Kaun blocked a shot. With 13 minutes, 22 seconds left, the Lumberjacks scored their first basket but the Jayhawks embarked on an 8-0 run highlighted by two three-pointers from Brandon Rush, who was playing in his second game of the season.

Offensively, Kansas was led by its big men. Sophomore Darrell Arthur scored 17 points and was eight of 10 from the field.

Jackson had 13 points and eight rebounds in just 15 minutes. Freshman point guard Tyrel Reed had eight points and five assists.

Final score
Kansas...................................**87**
Northern Arizona 46

Nov. 25, 2007

Arizona Wildcats

Allen Fieldhouse

Gut check

As the seconds ticked down in regulation, Brandon Rush fired a shot from beyond half court. Had he made it, the basket would have given the Kansas Jayhawks a victory in regulation – not to mention a highlight clip for the ages. But the ball clanged off the backboard, hung on the rim for what seemed like an eternity and then fell away. KU and the Wildcats were headed for overtime, and Coach Self was fine with the big tease.

"We needed to play five more competitive minutes like that," Self said, "to execute with the pressure on."

Matched against its best opponent since losing to UCLA in the NCAA regionals in March, KU struggled mightily much of the game to create offense. Self expressed his displeasure with the play of his guards, who failed time after time to get the ball inside to the post players. Still, KU forward Darrell Arthur had 20 points.

In addition, the Jayhawks were outrebounded by a startling margin of 38-29. The physical, foul-plagued game greatly resembled the season-ending loss to UCLA.

Kansas eventually won, thanks in large part to Rush, who took advantage of his second opportunity to be the hero. Rush had five points in the extra period – four on two emphatic slam dunks – and 17 overall. For the first time, he didn't look like the new Brandon Rush trying to do an impression of his old self. He was only supposed to play 20 minutes, but ended up playing 36 because freshman guard Tyrel Reed injured his ankle in the first half and his teammates couldn't stay out of foul trouble. The Jayhawks needed Rush to beat a Wildcats team that gave them a much-needed gut check.

Rush was back, but not all the way. He was not yet the defender he was a year ago. He struggled all night following Arizona sharpshooter Chase Budinger around screen after screen. Budinger had 27 points for the Wildcats.

In overtime, Budinger air-balled a three-point shot and fouled out. The KU fans waved good-bye.

Final score

Kansas.....................................**76**
Arizona 72

Brandon Rush shot over Daniel Dillon of Arizona in the first half.

Nov. 28, 2007

Florida Atlantic Owls

Allen Fieldhouse

Jackson steps up

For a coach, the natural reaction when a 6-foot-8 big man spots up from three-point range is to either cringe or motion to someone on the bench to take his warm-ups off and get to the scorer's table. Not so with Darnell Jackson, who swished a triple for the second time this year in Kansas' victory over Florida Atlantic.

His consistent outside shooting was just one of the reasons that Bill Self replaced Sasha Kaun with Jackson in the starting lineup against the Owls. Kaun had started 33 consecutive games.

"I think he's played well, and I think Sasha's labored," Self said.

Jackson had been aggressive with his improved jump shot all season. In the second half, he received a pass from Jeremy Case and didn't hesitate to shoot a three-pointer. He and the other big men practice it every day with KU assistant coach Danny Manning. In the drill, the forwards stand in a line and run to the high post where they have to shoot over the 6-foot-10 Manning. That has helped Jackson add more arc to his shot.

Against Florida Atlantic, KU was led in scoring by Brandon Rush, who scored 17 points for the second straight game in just 19 minutes of action.

Final score

Kansas.....................................87
Florida Atlantic 49

Top: Darnell Jackson joined the starting lineup against Florida Atlantic and in the opening minutes rejected a shot by the Owls' Carlos Monroe.

Left: Coming off the bench, Sasha Kaun got free for a dunk over Brett Royster as KU's Cole Aldrich watched.

17

Dec. 2, 2007

Southern California Trojans

Los Angeles

Hold the Mayo

His No. 32 jersey was flying off the shelves at $75 a pop and NBA scouts were in the house to see Ovinton J'Anthony Mayo, a 6-foot-5 scoring machine from Huntington, W. Va. They saw a lot of him. O.J. Mayo played all 40 minutes for Southern Californai against Kansas, but he finished with almost as many turnovers (five) as shots made (six) and his was the losing cause. In their first road game of the 2007-2008 season, the Jayhawks prevailed.

"I think we just proved that no one player can beat us," Kansas guard Mario Chalmers said. It was Chalmers who willed the offensively challenged Jayhawks to victory with 17 second-half points on the way to scoring 20 in the game. It was Chalmers' long three-pointer at the end of the shot clock in the game's final minute that kept KU from blowing an eight-point lead with two minutes left.

"We certainly made it very entertaining for fans," coach Bill Self said, "but that shouldn't happen with a veteran ball club."

The defeat of the Trojans was the Jayhawks' seventh straight victory, and second in a row against youthful and talented Pac-10 teams. Against Arizona, the Jayhawks struggled to contain forward Chase Budinger. Defending Mayo was a different assignment, one that required a guard quick enough to keep him from penetrating and long enough to contest his outside shot. In preparing for this game, Self knew that senior Russell Robinson was the man.

For 33 minutes, Robinson backed up his coach's faith. His only job was to keep an eye on that No. 32 jersey and make sure that Mayo had to work for every bucket. Mayor made some eye-opening plays that had scouts scribbling frantically, but his stat line wasn't overwhelming: 19 points on six-of-21 shooting, two assists, five turnovers.

"He didn't have his best game and still got 19," Robinson said. "He played 40 minutes. He was a little tired. He kind of settled for a lot of shots and made my job easier."

KU shot only 34 percent from the field in the first half, but because of its defense trailed only 27-25 at intermission. In the second half, with USC leading 32-29, Chalmers scored on two consecutive three-point plays, each time when he was fouled going for a fast-break layup. KU never lost the lead. The Trojans climbed within two points with 54 seconds left. Self called a timeout with 32 seconds left and drew up a play for Jackson inside. The play fell apart and Rodrick Stewart passed the ball to Chalmers behind the three-point line with three seconds on the shot clock. He jumped and nailed it, giving KU a 58-53 lead with 20 seconds left.

At that moment, the 9,000 or so USC fans went silent, and the stage at the Galen Center no longer belonged to Mayo. Chalmers showed once again that he shines under the late-game spotlight.

Southern California's star, O.J. Mayo, found himself caught between Kansas defenders Russell Robinson and Darrell Arthur.

Final score

Kansas..	**59**
Southern California	55

Southern California's Devon Jefferson was forced by Darnell Jackson and Sasha Kaun into taking a bad shot in the first half.

Dec. 5, 2007

Eastern Washington Eagles

Allen Fieldhouse

Attack, attack, attack!

At practice, Bill Self challenged KU's guards to get the ball inside to the big men. If they didn't, well, they would have plenty of time to think about it while doing some extra running. The Jayhawks, now ranked third in the country, proved that they could take a hint. As a result, KU big men Darrell Arthur and Darnell Jackson scored the Jayhawks' first 15 points in a pounding of Eastern Washington.

Jackson finished with 17 – mostly from around the basket – and Arthur added 15 with a variety of moves that showed off what the talented sophomore could do when he got going early.

Self had a simple message for the Jayhawks before their game against the Eagles of the Big Sky Conference: Attack, attack, attack!

"Mario and Rod and Russell just started the game off by throwing inside and getting easy baskets," Self said. Using Arthur's nickname, he continued, "The next thing you know, Shady's got his confidence, and we're on our way."

Arthur got his first bucket by spinning to the baseline for a layup. For his next trick, he pulled out the jump hook. Soon after, Arthur spun into the lane and hit a short jumper.

"We had a little more height," Arthur said, "so we just took advantage."

The Eagles' starting lineup has a 6-foot-4 power forward and a 6-8 center. Their tallest player was 6 feet 9.

Final score
Kansas....................................**85**
Eastern Washington...............47

Darrell Arthur shot over the smaller Eastern Washington defenders, above, and ended the game with 15 points. Darnell Jackson, left, led KU scorers with 17 points. On this dunk, left, the Eagles' Milan Stanojevic simply stayed out of the way.

Dec. 8, 2007

DePaul Blue Demons

Allen Fieldhouse

Together again

Sasha Kaun got angry, Sherron Collins got on the floor and the fans at Allen Fieldhouse got what they'd been looking for: an emphatic victory against a tough opponent. All game, steals and long rebounds turned into easy layups and alley-oops, and the fieldhouse rocked in appreciation.

For the first time all season, KU played with its full complement of stars. Collins, who had missed the previous six games recovering from surgery on his left foot, darted off the bench at the 14-minute mark of the first half, signaling his return. And Kaun played his best game of the year. The senior center had 15 points, five rebounds and two blocks in only 15 minutes.

Kaun, a two-year starter, lost his starting job to Darnell Jackson six games into the season. KU coach Bill Self hoped that the move would provide a spark to Kaun, who admitted on Saturday that he hadn't been focused in his final season.

"I just looked slow out there," he said, "going through the motions. I need to get more into the games and just have fun out there."

Kaun's day started much like his season. After a few minutes, he had compiled a foul, a missed layup and a turnover. Self replaced him with freshman Cole Aldrich, and Kaun was noticeably distraught on the bench.

When Darrell Arthur picked up his second foul with 10 minutes, 39 seconds left, Self subbed in Kaun, wondering how the 6-foot-11 Russian would respond. The Jayhawks were trailing 13-12, but Kaun started a massive turnaround with the first six points of a 24-1 KU run. The Jayhawks, 9-0, held the Blue Demons scoreless for almost 7 minutes at one point and led 39-22 at halftime. Kaun scored nine more points in the second half, going four of four from the field.

Collins, who led KU in scoring through two games at 16 a pop, wasn't at full strength and didn't have to be. Mario Chalmers and Robinson had things well under control. Chalmers, who is establishing himself as KU's Mr. Everything. had 12 points, nine rebounds, seven assists and seven steals. Robinson added nine assists and two steals.

"For the first time," Kaun said, "we were all together on the court. It's going to be a big change for us."

Said Collins, "It feels good to be complete again."

Final score

Kansas **84**
DePaul 66

DePaul's Dar Tucker, left, and Matija Poscic, right, put heavy pressure on Darnell Jackson. The referees called a tie on the play.

Collins' good fortune is KU's

KU was actually lucky that Collins missed only six games. If the team doctors hadn't caught the stress fracture in his left foot when they did, he might have broken it eventually and been out much longer.

Before the injury surfaced, Collins was hot, leading KU in scoring at 16 points a game through two games. He had spent the offseason getting in better shape after struggling with his fluctuating weight during a promising freshman season. He had stopped eating as much fast food and turned up the conditioning, and he looked good.

After all of that, Self wondered how Collins would handle the setback.

"I thought he really could go in the tank," Self said, "and he hasn't at all."

His return to health would make KU just about whole as a team. He was still not as quick as he was before, but there are things Collins can do that no one else can.

"He's the best pure creator on our team right now," guard Brandon Rush said. "He's crazy with that ball. He's got that ball on a yo-yo."

The main question about his time off was whether the weight he'd lost would magically reappear. Collins kept the weight off.

"I just wanted to show coach that I'm disciplined enough to do it," Collins said.

Collins had never missed this much court time, but he realized that the team benefited. The Jayhawks managed to stay unbeaten while getting Rodrick Stewart and Tyrel Reed more chances. Still, Collins' return was necessary for KU to evolve.

"We need to have him back so we can have a full arsenal," Self said. "We have a better chance to play closer to our potential now."

J. Brady McCollough

Dec. 15, 2007

Ohio Bobcats

Kansas City

A new home in Kansas City

In their first game at the new Sprint Center in downtown Kansas City, the Jayhawks made themselves right at home. Kansas City native Brandon Rush made sure of it.

Starting his first game of the season, Rush scored 11 points in the first 8 minutes and led the Jayhawks' clobbering of Ohio. After the game, he gave his hometown's new crown jewel a glowing recommendation:

"It's worth it, what they spent for it. I think it's probably the best arena I've been in a while. So much better than Kemper."

In recent years, when the Kansas Jayhawks boarded the bus to Kansas City, they honestly would have preferred to stay home. At three-decades old Kemper Arena in the West Bottoms, birds flew through the rafters and the floors were slippery. The building simply didn't inspire greatness. For Brandon Rush, Kemper was home court. But on this day, he came home to a place he could be proud of.

KU coach Bill Self had considered starting Rush in the DePaul game seven days before. After Rush was arrested for failure to attend two court dates for separate traffic violations, Self delayed that and Rodrick Stewart continued to start in his place.

Against an Ohio team that had won six games and lost three and was good enough to win at Maryland three days before, it was time. Rush went right to work, nailing two wide-open three-pointers for starters. Rush had said his shot looked better on video than it did last year – he spent hours in rehab doing shooting drills from a chair – and it looked as if it did.

After those first spectacular baskets, Rush drove to the basket and threw an over-the-shoulder, no-look pass to Darrell Arthur for an easy dunk. Then Rush was fouled and hit two free throws. After

another assist to Darnell Jackson on a lob, Rush had been involved in 12 of KU's first 14 points. He hit another three with 12:21 left, and KU went on a 19-0 run and took a 29-9 lead. At the half, it was 46-20.

Meanwhile, the Jayhawks were relentless on defense, holding Ohio to 17.2 percent shooting in the first half and 28.3 percent for the game. Rush was the hometown hero with his 13 points, but the starting lineup all contributed. Russell Robinson had 11 assists; Mario Chalmers had 17 points, five assists and four steals; Arthur had 14 points and eight rebounds and Jackson 11 points and eight rebounds.

When Ohio's Bert Whittington tried to escape from KU's Russell Robinson, above, right, he spun around and found himself head to head with Darrell Arthur. The Jayhawks' tough defense held the Bobcats to only 20 points in the first half.

Facing page, below right: Sasha Kaun hounded Michael Allen. Far right: As his father, Ronnie Chalmers, and his head coach Bill Self, looked on from the bench, Mario Chalmers went in for a layup.

Final score
Kansas 88
Ohio 51

Dec. 18, 2007

Georgia Tech Yellow Jackets
Atlanta

Tightening up on the road

The third-ranked Jayhawks remained undefeated against Georgia Tech, but after six weeks of their season, a pattern had developed in their road games. When Kansas went on the road, the home team was never out of the game.

In the second half at Anderson Memorial Coliseum in Atlanta, Kansas led by as many as 13 points and with 1:04 to play had an eight-point lead. By the end, they just escaped with a big road win over an ACC school.

Darnell Jackson and Darrell Arthur spent the game mired in foul trouble. Combined they played 40 minutes. KU's two best clutch free-throw shooters – Russell Robinson and Mario Chalmers – combined to go zero of three from the line in the last minute. Sherron Collins forgot to call timeout and instead turned the ball over underneath the Georgia Tech basket. But with 8 seconds left in the game, Collins did what Chalmers and Robinson couldn't. He hit two free throws and gave KU a three-point lead, 69-66.

Georgia Tech had possession and the length of the floor to go to tie the game with a three-pointer. Instead of demanding that KU foul to prevent a three-point attempt, Self left it up to his team.

"Coach," Robinson said, "let's defend it."

With Darnell Jackson fouled out of the game, Robinson didn't want to have to count on rebounding a missed free throw on the other end.

Georgia Tech inbounded the ball to point guard Matt Causey, who had slippery fingers the entire game. Pressured by Collins, Causey mishandled the ball at half-court. Collins swiped up the ball and raced down court for a layup as the clock was about to expire.

Final score
Kansas **71**
Georgia Tech 66

Maurice Miller of Georgia Tech was wrapped up Sherron Collins and Darnell Jackson.

Who's the man?

Kansas is undefeated this season, yet coach Bill Self wonders who his go-to guy is – and whether that's a good thing or a bad thing.

Through 11 games, the Jayhawks have had seven different players lead them in scoring. Self's first instinct is to say, "A lot of people would like to have that problem." Then, in midsentence, he decided it might actually be a problem. He considered the win at Georgia Tech. The Jayhawks played a strong game for the first 35 minutes. Point guard Russell Robinson was on his way to being the team's latest leading scorer. KU led by 13. Then the Jayhawks stagnated in their half-court offense.

As the Yellow Jackets climbed back into the game, KU needed baskets, but where would they come from? Brandon Rush was not being aggressive. Mario Chalmers and Darrell Arthur were in foul trouble and hadn't gotten into a flow. So the Jayhawks became content to run the clock. Georgia Tech pulled to within one point with 9 seconds left. Of course, KU won. Its balance is a big reason. But still, Self sees what can happen late in games with a group of players who have a tendency to defer to each other.

"At crunch time, with the (Chicago) Bulls, everybody knew who was getting the ball," Self said.

J. Brady Mccollough

Dec. 22, 2007

Miami (Ohio) RedHawks *Allen Fieldhouse*

Be efficient. Win.

The book on beating Bill Self's Kansas Jayhawks: Slow the game to a crawl. Work the shot clock and limit KU possessions. Don't let them run. Make them play in the halfcourt.

Miami of the Mid-American Conference came into Allen Fieldhouse knowing all that and had the pedigree to execute the plan. In a stretch of 44 games, the RedHawks hadn't allowed an opponent to crack 70 points. The Jayhawks prepared for a mudwrestling match, a test of wills.

Yet it wasn't like that. KU played its most efficient offensive game of the season, shooting 58 percent from the field, turning the ball over only six times — lowest of the season — and winning the game.

The Jayhawks, guard hit the 70 plateau with 3 minutes, 44 seconds left when Brandon Rush made a breakaway layup.

Coach Bill Self had built up the three-game stretch against Ohio, Georgia Tech and Miami to his team as the most crucial portion of its nonconference slate.

"Those were the three back-to-back-to-back in a seven-day period that would probably determine if we have a successful out-of-conference season," Self said.

KU's dodgy finish in Atlanta four days earlier was all but forgotten by this game. KU's big men, who were plagued by foul trouble against Georgia Tech, did most of the work against the diminutive RedHawks. Darrell Arthur, Darnell Jackson and Sasha Kaun scored 14 of the Jayhawks' first 20 points, springing KU to a 20-6 lead. In the second half, Arthur and Jackson combined for eight of KU's first 10, a sign that the Jayhawks' guards knew a good thing when they saw it and delivered the ball. Arthur finished with 14 points and 10 rebounds for his second double-double of the season. Jackson also finished with 14 points.

"We were dumping it down to them," Rush said. "We just let them work, let them have the floor."

Top: As four RedHawks looked on, Sasha Kaun hammered home a shot. Above: Rodrick Stewart drove through the Miami defense for a basket.

Final score

Kansas	**78**
Miami	54

Cole Aldrich thought he had a clean block on a shot by Yale's Travis Pinick, top, but the referee disagreed, calling him for a foul. The night belonged to Darnell Jackson, above, who scored 20 points.

Final score

Kansas **86**

Yale 53

Dec. 29, 2007

Yale Bulldogs *Allen Fieldhouse*

Grand theft

"Things have to go your way," KU guard Russell Robinson said after this game.

They did from the opening minutes and the third-ranked Jayhawks amassed a season-best 18 steals in running their record to 13-0 against Yale of the Ivy League.

Kansas had four steals – two by Robinson – before the first television timeout. Until the final minute, the Jayhawks had more steals than Yale had field goals. Eight players owned at least one steal.

The evening's most artistic swipe belonged to forward Darnell Jackson early in the second half. He cut off a passing lane, made the steal and then fumbled the ball, but recovered it on the wing in front of the Kansas bench. He cast his eyes on the basket, put a spin move on Yale guard Eric Flato, rolled in a layup and was fouled.

Although it's basketball nature to have adrenaline push the ball off target after a highlight-reel play, Jackson scored the free-throw. The play started a Jackson sequence of points and rebounds that made him the game's leading scorer with 20 and among the top rebounders with five.

The Jayhawks entered the week leading the Big 12 and ranked fourth nationally with 11.3 steals a game. Kansas had never averaged as many as 10 steals a game in a season since the statistic became official in the mid-1970s.

The team has a few rules when it comes to steal attempts. Don't try it with fewer than 10 seconds remaining on the shot clock. Take chances farther away from the basket. And figure out early how tightly the game is being called by the referees.

Robinson's disruptions caused Yale to alter its attack and contributed to the Bulldogs' 37 percent shooting.

"You know you've got it turned up when they start sending their forwards to the backcourt to set picks," Robinson said.

Jan. 5, 2008

Boston College Eagles
Chestnut Hill, Mass.

The big men score

Darrell Arthur was expected to score points. Unexpected was the emergence of Darnell Jackson. The two KU big men scored 22 and 25 points, respectively, in Kansas' pasting of Boston College. In as dominant a post performance as KU had seen in years, the Eagles had no answer.

"That's what we've said all along," coach Bill Self said. "In a broken-floor game, we're going to look pretty good because we've got guys that can run and jump. But in a grind-it-out, halfcourt game, you gotta be able to throw it in the post and get a basket."

KU did that Saturday early and often. Jackson and Arthur combined to shoot 19 of 25 from the floor and nine of 10 from the free-throw line. Just as they had in games at Southern California and Georgia Tech, the Jayhawks fell into a lull after taking a 25-point lead 4 minutes into the second half. This time, they snapped out of it quickly.

Boston College had gone on an 11-point run when guard Mario Chalmers exchanged words with Boston College's Rakim Sanders. Then Chalmers jawed with the referee, who threw some choice words back at him. Arthur closed his eyes, clinched his fists and yelled.

"Adrenaline just starts running through your body," Arthur said, "and makes you just want to go at them."

The Jayhawks knew where to go. They ran a simple pick-and-roll play for Jackson that resulted in a layup, kicking off an 8-0 run that put the game out of reach. This was the second straight game in which Jackson led KU in scoring. His 25 points was a career high, and he added nine rebounds.

Final score

Kansas **85**

Boston College 60

Surrounded by Jayhawk defenders, Rakim Sanders of Boston College tried to take a shot. Darrell Arthur, Brandon Rush and Mario Chalmers were there to deny Sanders the opportunity.

No. 3 and you hadn't noticed?

After the Boston College game, Self recalled a conversation with a reporter for a national outlet who said, "Well, now we have to consider you among the better teams."

"I was going, 'I thought we were among the better teams before you saw us play,'" Self said, laughing. "A lot of it is location, let's be honest. We go play Boston College, and you've got every major East Coast writer at that game."

Jan. 8, 2008

Loyola (Maryland) Greyhounds

Allen Fieldhouse

Killer instinct... missing

According to their coach, the Kansas Jayhawks played Loyola without two of their top players.

Mario Chalmers was out with an injured groin. Brandon Rush played, but KU's leading scorer the last two years shot the ball seven times and scored nine points in a nondescript outing, nearly missing in action. At halftime, KU coach Bill Self delivered Rush a message: Be more aggressive.

"A coach should never have to tell his leading scorer the past two years to be aggressive," Self said. "But we have to do that way too often."

On the other hand, Self rarely has to say such things to Sherron Collins, who scored 18 points in 28 minutes of the KU victory. Collins started the game in place of Chalmers and gave third-ranked KU, now 15-0 for the season, a boost. They needed it. In a sluggish first half, the Jayhawks led only 26-22 with 5:08 to go. Collins had 11 points in the first half, equaling his best output for an entire game since returning from a stress fracture in his left foot in early December.

"This is the best I've felt by far since I've been back," Collins said. "In practice, there's no pain at all. I'm able to do everything."

When Collins is doing everything, magic is possible any time he touches the ball. His teammates compare his skill with the ball to a yo-yo.

"I think he's getting closer to being 100 percent," Self said. "I think he's real close. It's unfortunate that Mario tweaked his groin, but probably fortunate for Sherron.."

As for Rush, health no longer seemed to be a question. It's the same old story, according to Self, who has been trying to instill in Rush a killer instinct since he arrived on campus. Yet at halftime, Rush

Yo-yo man: Sherron Collins, recovering nicely from injuries earlier in the season, looked for a passing opportunity while he was covered by Loyola's Marquis Sullivan.

had only three points. Self challenged him to do more, and Rush scored six unanswered points early in the second half. Then he disappeared again.

"We're not going to be a really good team unless he plays to his talent level offensively," Self said. "He can do a better job. He'd be the first to tell you that, but for whatever reason, he shies away from shooting the ball."

Final score
Kansas **90**
Loyola 60

Jan. 12, 2008

Nebraska Cornhuskers

Lincoln, Neb.

Which Rush would it be?

One of two scenarios played out in Kansas' win over Nebraska.

Scenario one: Brandon Rush, a 22-year-old college kid who was called out by his coach for not being aggressive enough, decided that for the rest of the season he would attack. So he went out and scored 19 points against the Cornhuskers.

Scenario two: Rush hit a couple of threes early, his confidence soared and he kept shooting. His 19 points amounted to a one-night stand, no forecast for the rest of the season, only Rush's turn to lead the ultra-balanced Jayhawks in scoring.

In the first scenario, Bill Self was a master puppeteer who turned his reluctant star into the player everyone wanted him to be. In the second, Rush would go back to being simply a talented role player.

Naturally, knowing which was which would take many more games. For this night, Self and the Jayhawks would have to be satisfied with Rush's effort, his best since returning from surgery on a torn right ACL. Besides the points, Rush added six rebounds, four assists and three steals for KU, which won its 17th straight conference opener.

The Jayhawks, favorites to win their fourth straight Big 12 title, started their 2008 campaign against what was supposed to be a much-improved Nebraska team, a squad with high-quality wins over Pac-10 programs Oregon and Arizona State. Accordingly, the Bob Devaney Sports Center was packed with 13,000 upset-hungry fans. KU played in front of large patches of crimson and blue in its first three away games at Southern California, Georgia Tech and Boston College, but there was no such cheering section 200 miles away in Lincoln.

As techno music blared at the game's start, the public address announcer bellowed, "Husker fans, the entire nation is watching you live on ESPN right now!"

The place went nuts – until Rush quickly took over. He scored eight points in the game's first 5 minutes and gave KU a 14-5 lead. KU went to the half ahead 42-30. The rave-like atmosphere was quieted.

As for his coach's challenge earlier in the week, Rush said, "that's going to be the last time (Self) ever says something to me about being aggressive."

Down the hall inside the Devaney Center, Rush's friend, Mario Chalmers, wasn't so sure. Asked whether he thought this would be the last time Self would have to publicly question Rush's aggressiveness, Chalmers paused and thought for about five seconds.

"I don't believe it," Chalmers said. "But I hope it's the last time."

Final score

Kansas **79**

Nebraska 58

Before a fired-up crowd at the Devaney Center, Nebraska's Aleks Maric jumped to block Brandon Rush's jump shot. Rush made more than he missed, scoring 19 points.

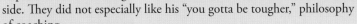

At last, his kind of team

When he arrived at Kansas, Bill Self found that some players were still upset about the departure of Roy Williams, and they took Self all wrong. They didn't like the way he challenged them. They did not seem to respond to his fun-loving side. They did not especially like his "you gotta be tougher," philosophy of coaching.

Self tried to adjust, players tried to adjust, but it just wasn't quite right. Those Jayhawks won games, won Big 12 championships – they were awfully good teams – but they lost in March, and Self just felt like he wasn't getting through.

If Bill Self could make a sketch of his kind of team, it would look a lot like these 2008 Jayhawks. They're deep – already they've had seven different players lead the team in scoring. They're intense – they have held opponents to 37 percent shooting this year. They're unselfish – they lead the Big 12 in assists and nobody seems unhappy, even though nobody on this talent-laden team is averaging 30 minutes per game.

Everything works with these guys. Of course, it doesn't hurt to have five McDonald's High School All-Americans, but it's more than just talent. This team connects. The players like each other. They can play any number of styles. This team can shoot, can run, can press, can dominate a half-court game. This has always been a Bill Self dream – to coach a team that can beat you any way you want to play.

"You usually have a team that's missing something," Self says. "You wish that you had one more shooter or one more post player. This team, the pieces just all fit together."

And this team might be the first team to get Bill Self unfiltered. He doesn't hold back. He's unleashing his real voice.

Those players have been through all that with Bill Self. This is his fifth year at Kansas, so this is his team, fully and completely. He recruited them all, developed them all, he has watched them all grow up, he has helped them through hard times and gotten mad at them when they backed down and celebrated with them in the good moments. Self has won with a lot of teams. But now, Self is building his team.

And he is amazed to find that they think like him. They brag about their defense – Self loves tough defense. They are intense at the right times – Self prizes intensity above almost anything else. But they also have fun at the right time.

"We just feed off of coach," Darrell Arthur says. "We're at a point now where we have a pretty good idea what he wants from us, and we just go out and do that."

Joe Posnanski

Jan. 14, 2008

Oklahoma Sooners
Allen Fieldhouse

Mr. Outside and his Inside pals

Brandon Rush kept it going against Oklahoma, scoring 16 points and grabbing 9 rebounds and helping the Jayhawks blow away the ordinarily tough Sooners. For the second straight game, he looked like the smooth-shooting kid who led KU in scoring his first two years on campus. Over the two games, Rush hit nine of 14 three-pointers.

As he did against Nebraska in Lincoln, Rush got going early, hitting three of five in the first half.

The Jayhawks showed they could play inside, too. Darnell Jackson had 17 points and eight rebounds, and Darrell Arthur added 14 points and eight rebounds. This game was supposed to be a test for KU's big men, who would be going against talented freshman Blake Griffin and much-improved senior Longar Longar. But when Griffin was injured 5 minutes into the game, it left Longar to deal with Arthur and Jackson by himself. Longar finished the game with 21 points, but that was all the short-handed Sooners had to offer.

"I was kind of disappointed (by Griffin's injury)," Jackson said. "I was really looking forward to playing against him."

Beating teams the way the Jayhawks have — they had won their first 17 games by an average of 26 points — it was natural to get excited for any actual competition.

For the first time since the beginning of the season, all the student seats were filled, a sign that Kansas' amazing football season was past, that classes were about to begin and the key part of the basketball season had arrived.

Final score

Kansas **85**

Oklahoma 55

One of his game-high nine rebounds, Brandon Rush grabbed this one away from the Sooners' Taylor Griffin.

Darrell Arthur shucked Oklahoma's Austin Johnson out of the way, above, and grabbed one of his five first-half rebounds. Below: Russell Robinson made life miserable for the Sooners' Omar Leary.

Nothing missing here

Even before Oklahoma's prized freshman, Blake Griffin, left the game because of a knee injury, Kansas had begun the process of destroying the Sooners. Kansas' defense is its No. 1 weapon, and it suffocated Oklahoma's scorers for the first 10 minutes. Griffin played only 5 of those minutes before limping into the locker room. When he left, the Sooners were down 11-2, and he'd missed both shots he'd taken.

Kansas' lead eventually ballooned to 20-4 8 minutes, 30 seconds into the game. Guards Russell Robinson and Mario Chalmers, with their quick feet and even quicker hands, set a nasty and pesky tone on the perimeter, and they were backed by quick and long leapers Darrell Arthur, Darnell Jackson and Sasha Kaun. Kansas' defensive flexibility and capability almost seems unfair, especially when the opposition loses its best offensive player.

The Jayhawks are nearly as impressive on the opposite end of the court. With Brandon Rush, Chalmers and Sherron Collins, Kansas has an easy bailout when its offense breaks down. Rush, Chalmers or Collins will simply throw in a long three-pointer when the shot clock drips below 10 seconds. Arthur and Jackson play off each other quite well in the paint. They both can step out and hit the 15-footer. Arthur has developed a solid back-to-the-basket game. Jackson cleans up on garbage buckets.

I can't find a hole in this team.

Jason Whitlock

Jan. 19, 2008

Missouri Tigers
Columbia, Mo.

Winning in the House of Horrors

If there was ever a team ripe for an upset on the road against its bitter rival, it was the Kansas Jayhawks at Mizzou Arena. Their leading scorer in conference play started the game so cold he could have been a thermometer outside. They were called for 12 fouls in the first half, created only five turnovers and led by just two at intermission. But KU simply found a way. And the Jayhawks had to do it on the road, in a city that had traditionally been a House of Horrors for undefeated Kansas teams.

"The key to having a great season is to win games when you don't play your best," coach Bill Self said. "And that's going to happen 10 times a year, and you gotta find a way to go 8-2 in those type of games to have a great season."

Against Missouri, the gut-check started when Kansas fell behind 7-1 early. It wasn't easy to make up that deficit, especially the way junior guard Brandon Rush started the game. Rush, who had led KU in two Big 12 games with 17.5 points a game, missed his first six shots, including four open threes, and was noticeably frustrated by his inaccuracy. Rush's night and the way he recovered turned out to be a fitting metaphor for Kansas' scrappy win. He finished with 13 points and nine rebounds and helped ice the game with four free throws in the game's final 2 minutes. Rush made nine of a career-high 14 attempts from the line.

"There are some players that have to make shots to play well," Self said. "For him, I think he still can play well and not make shots. I'm proud of his aggressiveness."

Mario Chalmers finished with 18 points, leading KU. Darnell Jackson and Darrell Arthur added 13 and 10, respectively.

For Missouri, it was a disappointing night, an opportunity lost. KU outrebounded Missouri 52-43 and had no players foul out despite the tight officiating; Missouri's Leo Lyons and Jason Horton both fouled out.

"I think we're the best team in the nation," guard Russell Robinson said. "Hopefully, later in the season we can decide that."

Final score

Kansas **76**
Missouri 70

Too big, too tall: Darrell Arthur shot over Missouri's Darryl Butterfield.

Airborne in Mizzou Arena, Sherron Collins finished a reverse layup in front of Missouri's Leo Lyons and Keon Lawrence.

Late in the game, Mario Chalmers drove on Missouri's Stefhon Hannah, and Hannah was called for a foul.

All sped up

The Jayhawks entered the game against Missouri first in field-goal percentage nationally at 52.3 percent, yet they shot only 40 percent against MU. How in the world was KU so cold?

"Mizzou had us sped up to the point we couldn't execute very well," coach Bill Self said. "We tried to make great plays instead of letting the ball make plays for us."

The Tigers, who normally play a full-court defense, hung back against the run-happy Jayhawks. KU guard Brandon Rush said it was their mixture of pressure and a 2-3 zone that kept Kansas off balance most of the game. The result of MU's defensive plan: KU finished the game with only two fast-break points.

J. Brady McCollough

DeMarre Carroll, top, did what he could to prevent Sasha Kaun from getting an easy shot. Nearby were the Tigers' Leo Lyons and KU's Brandon Rush.

Jan. 19, 2008

Missouri Tigers

Columbia, Mo.

That was a foul? Missouri Coach Mike Anderson, above left, begged to differ. Above right: Stefhon Hannah was caught between Sherron Collins, left, and Darnell Jackson, right.

The future sits on the bench

Reed

Aldrich

Hanging out in their apartment at Jayhawker Towers, Kansas freshmen Cole Aldrich and Tyrel Reed couldn't help but think about things to come. This far into the 2007-08 season, they had barely been tested. Aldrich, a center, was averaging 9.2 minutes a game and Reed, a guard, 8.8.

"We know it's going to come sooner or later," Reed said.

Unlike freshmen at KU in past years, Aldrich and Reed had been able to focus on improving in practice instead of putting any freshman flaws on display in front of thousands at Allen Fieldhouse. It's a luxury afforded freshmen on the deep and experienced No. 2 team in the country.

Aldrich, who struggled early on adapting to the speed of the college game, looked more comfortable after three Big 12 games. He grabbed 10 rebounds in 26 total minutes to go

along with eight points and four blocks. Most important, Aldrich played key stretches against some of the league's best big men – Aleks Maric of Nebraska, Longar Longar of Oklahoma and DeMarre Carroll of Missouri – and held his own. Aldrich even received a lob against MU and threw it down for an easy dunk. Aldrich said he got the most out of his 13 minutes against Longar.

"I proved to myself that I can hang with the big boys in the conference," Aldrich said.

Reed, a native of Burlington, Kan., started the season impressively, getting playing time thanks to the injuries to Brandon Rush and Sherron Collins. But he had seen little action since suffering an ankle injury against Arizona on Nov. 25.

J. Brady McCollough

Jan. 23, 2008

Iowa State Cyclones
Allen Fieldhouse

19 straight and rolling

What's a coach to do when his team is charging along like a cross-country train? At a practice before this game, Kansas coach Bill Self had to do something. So when he saw a brief lapse in execution, he jumped on it.

"I went nuts on our guys for a few minutes," Self said, "just because I hadn't gone nuts on them in a long time."

During that tirade, Self shot a glance at senior forward Darnell Jackson, who was smiling.

"Darnell," Self said, "knew exactly what I was doing."

Jackson knew that Self was simply trying to get KU's attention, and he responded with the same ease in practice that he displayed this night in KU's victory over Iowa State. Jackson scored 21 points and added 11 rebounds for the Jayhawks, who won their 19th straight game.

Like Jackson, the rest of the Jayhawks were letting nothing get under their skin, no matter what opponents tried. For this game, Iowa State came in with the same plan that allowed Missouri to hang tough with the normally high-flying Jayhawks. KU had only two fast-break points against the Tigers, and the Cyclones were going to do whatever they could to keep the Jayhawks from running.

"Teams are sending one to the glass and sending four back," forward Darrell Arthur said. "It's pretty tough getting fast-break points."

It was tough on KU's guards but it gave Jackson and Arthur free rein inside, and the Cyclones paid dearly. The two big men combined to shoot 17 of 27 from the field and did it from outside and inside. Arthur finished the game with 16 points to go with Jackson's 21. Iowa State held KU to seven fast-break points, but what did it accomplish in the end?

"Everyone tries to take something away," Self said.

Because Iowa State neglected to trap KU's big men in the post, they began to treat it like a practice session. Assistant coach Danny Manning spent the night challenging Arthur to try different moves and keep the Cyclones' defenders guessing.

Arthur injured his calf muscle in practice and played tentatively in the first two minutes before Self pulled him. When Arthur came back in, he was a different player.

Self also shed light on Sherron Collins' two-point performance by saying that Collins had turned his right ankle in practice.

Final score

Kansas **83**
Iowa State 59

Darrell Arthur battled two Iowa State players for a loose ball, above. Not long into the game, coach Bill Self made it clear how he felt about an official's call, left.

Jan. 26, 2008

Nebraska Cornhuskers
Allen Fieldhouse

Grand Canyon

Kansas center Sasha Kaun, not known for his quick and nimble hands, picked the pocket of Nebraska point guard Cookie Miller beyond the three-point line. Twice.

Soon after, 6-foot-9 forward Darrell Arthur took 6-foot-4 Nebraska guard Ryan Anderson off the dribble and was fouled.

KU administered its second thrashing of Nebraska in as many weeks, and the gulf between the teams looked something like the Grand Canyon. KU led 44-15 at halftime and rendered the second half irrelevant.

"We try not to focus on how much we're winning by, because sometimes we'll lose focus," forward Darnell Jackson said. "We always say: The second-half score is zero-zero. We try to play like we're down 10, and then we have to come back."

The Jayhawks held the Cornhuskers to 20.7 percent shooting and six field Rush each almost outscored Nebraska with 14 points apiece in the opening 20 minutes. KU had 12 assists compared with the Huskers' one? Nebraska center Aleks Maric, averaging 16.6 points a game, was so overmatched that he finished with a goose egg.

To Self, it was simple. KU played with an enthusiasm he thought was lacking in its last game against Iowa State – one in which the margin of victory was 24 points.

Against Nebraska, KU had 14 steals, four of which came at the hands of point guard Russell Robinson.

"Our energy level was better," Self said. "Russell did a good job of heating up the ball up top. He created a lot of havoc."

Final score

Kansas **84**

Nebraska 49

Dishing out KU's second husking of Nebraska in the season, Darrell Arthur finished a dunk and Darnell Jackson stood ready to go back on defense.

Coming up: "A real challenge"

After his team defeated Nebraska, coach Bill Self was noticeably excited about the next game, against Kansas State in Manhattan, Kan.

"We'll have to play at a level that we haven't played at here in the last few weeks," he said. "They're playing through two guys that are as talented as any two guys on the same team, maybe in the country."

He referred to freshmen Michael Beasley and Bill Walker. Beasley was the 6-foot-9 power forward who said in summer 2007 that K-State would beat KU in Manhattan, Lawrence or Africa.

"He's a tough player," KU's

Sherron Collins said. "But for him to go out and say something like that ... We're not going to respond back to him. Just gonna let our game talk for us."

Self said he didn't mind Beasley's guarantee.

"When a guy is averaging 24 (points) and 13 (rebounds), I think he has a right to talk a little bit."

Like KU, K-State was unbeaten in conference play.

"We're ready," said Collins, "for a real challenge."

J. Brady McCollough

Jan. 30, 2008

Kansas State Wildcats
Manhattan, Kan.

Falling back to earth

Mario Chalmers walked off the Bramlage Coliseum floor, his fists clinched in anger as Kansas State students flooded past him. Sherron Collins needed an escort. He kept his head down as teammate Brady Morningstar put his arm around him and walked him off the court. Russell Robinson and Brandon Rush didn't show any emotion whatsoever, their eyes focused straight ahead.

Each of Kansas' guards took their first loss of the season – KU's first loss at K-State since 1983 – a different way. But they all knew what happened in the defeat.

"We should have been more poised," said Collins. "We rushed shots a lot and (made) bad passes. We just made bad decisions. Tonight they were more poised than we were."

KU's guards were supposed to win this one for the No. 2 Jayhawks, who were now 20-1 for the season. They had played in so many big games just like this one, tasted defeat together on the brink of the Final Four in 2007. Their veteran leadership on the perimeter would be KU's best chance to counter K-State freshmen big men Michael Beasley and Bill Walker.

Yet Jacob Pullen, a freshman guard for K-State outshined KU's backcourt. Pullen scored 20 points and the Wildcats' ball-handlers turned over the ball only five times. The Jayhawks' patented pressure defense barely dented K-State.

KU's guards turned it over eight times – not an alarming statistic – but didn't make the most of numerous opportunities when they got into the lane. Rush said that the Jayhawks responded to K-State's hot shooting from three by trying to get baskets back quickly.

"We had some guys trying to do the right thing, but they weren't percentage plays at all," coach Bill Self said. Rush, meanwhile, had 12 first-half points and finished with 15, acknowledged his own failing: "I wasn't staying aggressive like I was supposed to."

"This stings more than what most would sting," Self said. "We have a really nice team. We do a lot of good things. But we weren't going to run the table. As much as I wish we could, that wasn't going to happen. This could be very good for us in the long run, but certainly it stings."

Final score
Kansas State **84**
Kansas 75

With Darnell Jackson in his face, K-State's Michael Beasley took an off-balance shot in the first half, above. Things improved for Beasley in the second half. Below: When he wasn't scoring, K-State guard Jacob Pullen played tight defense on KU's Russell Robinson.

Mugging for the camera and waving rubber chickens in scorn of the Jayhawks, the K-State faithful vented after the Wildcats ended not only KU's long winning streak in Manhattan but also its undefeated season.

Bill Self had a difficult time containing his frustration with the way this game went. Right: Clent Stewart, left, and Michael Beasley stripped the ball from Sasha Kaun. Throughout the night they gave KU's big men fits.

A sea of purple descended on the Bramlage court, dwarfing the Wildcat players.

Once victory was in hand, K-State coach Frank Martin broke a smile.

How the streak was broken

So much had been made about the streak, KU's string of 24 straight victories over K-State in Manhattan. Now, it could be used in the past tense. In the process, K-State proved that the only thing that mattered was the here and now.

"I've got nine first-year guys that have grown up a whole lot since November," K-State Coach Frank Martin said.

The Wildcats played as a tight, well-drilled unit when it counted. K-State led by as many as 12 points in the second half and withstood a KU charge. The Jayhawks pulled within 61-55, but the Wildcats had an answer. K-State countered with freshmen Michael Beasley (25 points) and reserve freshman guard Jacob Pullen, who scored 20.

"I knew my team was capable of beating anybody," said Beasley. "We showed it tonight. We just knocked off a Final Four-caliber team."

Martin said a key was dragging KU's big men out to the perimeter, and minimizing turnovers. The Wildcats accomplished both, getting Darrell Arthur in early foul trouble. K-State totaled only 13 turnovers compared with the Jayhawks' 16.

The defense also sparked K-State. KU shot 42.3 percent in the second half, quite a drop from its 53.6 percent effort in the first. It also outrebounded KU, 34-30. Jayhawks coach Bill Self credited the Wildcats with forcing his team to speed up, perhaps panic, if that's possible for such an experienced group.

"From the tip," Walker said about the turning point. "We showed we weren't going to back down and let them do what they wanted to do."

Howard Richman

The 'Cats were for real

K-State's victory was no fluke. The Wildcats were the superior team from start to finish. Beasley and Walker, while not on top of their games, were the two best players to take the court, and their presence – along with a hostile, energized crowd – elevated the performance of K-State's supporting cast.

The second-ranked Jayhawks simply failed to match K-State's emotion and energy. They were a step slow closing out on K-State's three-point shooters, and their alleged backcourt advantage never materialized because Mario Chalmers and Russell Robinson didn't pressure KSU's ballhandlers.

The vicious crowd, plus Beasley and Walker, turned Bill Self's Jayhawks extremely timid. The Jayhawks played scared.

Foul trouble limited Darrell Arthur to just 17 minutes. Darnell Jackson, KU's season-long surprising inside force, took two shots and grabbed four rebounds. Sasha Kaun managed to hit his lone shot attempt.

Did Jackson, Kaun and Arthur back away from the challenge presented by KSU's NBA-ready, physically mature big men? Or did KU's guards fail to get their bigs involved?

"We didn't play as well as we have been inside," Self said after the game. "Timid is too strong of a word, though." Jackson added: "I played offbeat a little bit. I had been used to getting the ball a lot. I didn't play well on the defensive end."

Beasley opened the game poorly, going scoreless for 10 minutes while throwing up an assortment of air balls and awkward shots. By the second half, he found his stroke, nailing three three-pointers and scoring 17 points. He finished with 25. Walker tossed in 22. He used his superior quickness and strength to drive past Jackson and Arthur and finish at the rim. Had he avoided launching a half-dozen terrible three-pointers, the Wildcats might've won by 20.

Honestly, had Beasley and Walker brought their A games, it would've been a slaughter.

Jason Whitlock

Part one of his guarantee was fulfilled and Michael Beasley led the celebration, above. Early in his time at K-State Beasley had said that the Wildcats would beat KU in Manhattan, in Lawrence, and even in Africa. Right: For KU, the night went like this shot by Russell Robinson – smacked down by K-State's Dominique Sutton.

Feb. 2, 2008

Colorado Buffaloes
Boulder, Colo.

No pity

His team was tied at halftime against Colorado, which was far behind KU in the Big 12 standings, and coach Bill Self had a message for the Kansas players:

"What's deep in your gut, go down there and find it. Find out who you are."

Only three days after their deflating loss to Kansas State, the Jayhawks clearly needed the introspection. Self wasn't going to let KU's special season begin to slip away here at the foot of the Rockies.

"Nobody," Self continued, "is throwing a pity party for you because you lost a game."

With Self's words fresh in their minds, the Jayhawks ran away from Colorado in the second half. And maybe, somewhere along the line, they stopped pitying themselves.

"Coach Self changed it at halftime," guard Sherron Collins said. It didn't hurt that Self also mentioned K-State's shocking loss at Missouri earlier in the day. Beating the Buffaloes meant that KU would head into its next game against Missouri with a half-game lead in the league standings. Simply put, it was a gift – one that the Jayhawks didn't seem intent on accepting in the first half.

After only four minutes had been played, the K-State score was announced over the loudspeaker at the Coors Events Center. Thousands of Kansas fans attending erupted, the first sign that Colorado's home arena would be turned once again this season into Allen Fieldhouse West. Colorado led 10-6 at that point, and the crimson and blue faithful assumed that the Jayhawks would start a rout. But even the first-place fruit dangling in front of the Jayhawks wasn't enough for them to wake up from their Manhattan, Kan., hangover right away.

KU played sluggishly, turning the ball over 10 times in the first half and shooting one of six three-pointers. On the other end, Colorado did what it wanted offensively, shooting 50 percent from the field and turning it over five times. KU went to the half tied 30-30.

Self told the Jayhawks that they needed to stop forcing things and make the easy play. The change was immediate in the second half. KU started on an 8-0 run. Then, the Jayhawks started to look like themselves again, the high-flying, in-your-face, dunking Jayhawks.

After the game, there was a sense of relief outside the Kansas locker room. But Darnell Jackson, who led KU with 18 points, wasn't going to feel too comfortable – not yet, anyway.

"No relief at all," he said. "We gotta stay hungry."

Final score

Kansas **72**

Colorado 59

Going for it: An active Brandon Rush dunked over Dwight Thorne II of Colorado, above, and grabbed a rebound from Caleb Patterson, facing page.

A concerned parent

Junior guard Brandon Rush said that his mother, Glenda Rush, called him after the Kansas State loss and told him he needed to go to the basket more. Against Colorado, Rush had an aggressive second half, getting to the free-throw line four times and finishing with 15 points.

Feb. 4, 2008

Missouri Tigers

Allen Fieldhouse

Another big man

For the second time in three games, Darrell Arthur, the talented centerpiece of Kansas' halfcourt offense, faced as much trouble with referees as he did with the Jayhawks' opponent. Arthur, a 6-foot-9 forward, was called for three fouls in the first half against Missouri, played only two minutes of the half and didn't start the second.

Enter Cole Aldrich, the 6-foot-11 freshman from Minnesota, who clearly was up to the challenge of the rivalry game. No KU player was more vital to the Jayhawks' whipping of Missouri

He gave the Jayhawks six points and nine rebounds in 12 minutes of playing time, and for the second straight year Kansas swept the regular-season series from Missouri. In the process, KU coach Bill Self found himself a fourth big man.

Arthur's foul trouble had rendered his talents useless for a large chunk of the last three games. But it opened the door for Aldrich, the McDonald's All-American who struggled with the speed of the college game earlier in the season.

When Aldrich entered the game in the first minute of the second half, he ran a pick-and-roll with guard Mario Chalmers on his first play. Chalmers overthrew Aldrich, but the fact that Chalmers threw it at all showed how much confidence Aldrich had built with his teammates. Aldrich pointed at Chalmers, who gave him a pat on the rear. No big deal; he'd get another chance. Sure enough, minutes later, Aldrich grabbed two offensive rebounds in a row and was fouled going up after the second. He coolly sank both free throws – he was four for four from the line in the game.

The Jayhawks were led by Brandon Rush's 19 points, which tied his season-high. They also outrebounded the Tigers 47-25.

Missouri played with four of the players who had been suspended for either breaking curfew or being involved in an incident at a night club in Columbia. A fifth player, Stefhon Hannah, suffered a broken jaw in the incident and was out for the season.

As for KU's Arthur, when he was on the floor he was supremely effective. He finished the game with13 points and six rebounds, showing what he could be when present.

Final score
Kansas **90**
Missouri 71

Above: One KU fan's take on the Tigers. Right: Russell Robinson rejected a shot by Missouri's Keon Lawrence. Below: Darnell Jackson finished a dunk.

Facing page: Missouri's Leo Lyons found himself wedged betweeen Darnell Jackson and Cole Aldrich as he tried to get a shot off.

Feb. 9, 2008

Baylor Bears

Allen Fieldhouse

Up and running again

In the first half of the Big 12 season, Kansas' opponents did everything they could to make sure the Jayhawks didn't run. The reason was never more clear than on this night. In an up-tempo game forced by Baylor's free-wheeling guards, KU flew up and down the floor in the second half and finally put away the Bears.

The Jayhawks hit triple digits on the scoreboard without making a three-point shot.

"That's unbelievable," KU coach Bill Self said. It was the first time in 271 games KU had not made a three-point shot, dating to 2000.

"It was like playing in the old days without the three-point line," imagined Darrell Arthur.

It was like heaven for guard Sherron Collins, who would take it back to the playground every night if he could. Collins was the key for Kansas, which scored 64 points and turned the ball over only once in the second half.

Through eight grueling Big 12 games, KU had been forced by its opponents to shed its running game and try to excel in the half-court. Thanks to the collective green-light mentality of Baylor's guards, the floodgates opened up for the Jayhawks. Collins scored 13 of his 17 points in the second half.

"Running," Collins said with a smile, "that's all I like to do is run. I can play a game like this any time."

In the first half, however, things were much slower and for only the second time this season, the Jayhawks were in danger of suffering defeat on their home floor. At the 16:24 mark, Baylor took a 10-4 lead – at that point the largest deficit for KU at Allen Fieldhouse all season. At halftime KU led only 36-33.

The stage was set for the track meet. KU, which had struggled to create offense with its defense of late, broke the game open with nine minutes left, leading 61-56. An Arthur block led to a Collins layup on the other end. A Collins defensive rebound turned into a layup by Brandon Rush, who played without a knee brace for the first time this season. A Chalmers steal became another Collins layup. Suddenly, Kansas led by 11, and Collins was just getting started.

"We lost the game because of transition defense," Baylor coach Scott Drew said. "We saw them go to another level."

The 20 fast-break points helped, but they weren't the only reason Kansas scored so easily. In the second half, the Jayhawks committed only one turnover. For the game, they made 36 of 46 free throws. Arthur stayed out of foul trouble, playing 33 minutes with 23 points and 10 rebounds, and Robinson had a season-high 22 points.

In a tempo tailor-made for him, Sherron Collins ran the court and laid in a basket.

Final score
Kansas **100**
Baylor 90

Brandon Rush slashed his way between Baylor's Curtis Jerrells and Henry Dugat, above, and battled for a loose ball with Aaron Bruce, below. Darrell Arthur, below right, put an abrupt halt to a drive by Dugat.

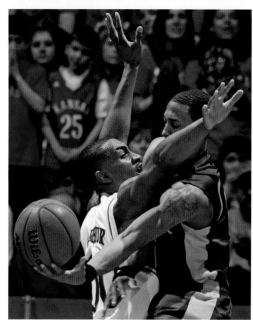

You can't mean that, ref! Coach Bill Self showed his displeasure at a call in the first half, left. Mario Chalmers and Russell Robinson battled the Longhorns' D. J. Augustin for a loose ball, below, but Augustin won.

Feb. 11, 2008

Texas Longhorns
Austin, Texas

Brought low again

It all happened so fast at the end. Texas' D.J. Augustin missed a free throw that could have iced the game. Russell Robinson snagged the rebound. Eight seconds were left, and coach Bill Self had already relayed the play that could keep his team rolling in the Big 12.

Robinson was supposed to go right, hand the ball off to Chalmers going to his left, and Chalmers would have the option of getting it to Brandon Rush coming off a couple of screens. But little of that happened, and Chalmers missed an awkward three-point attempt at the buzzer.

"Bad possession," Self said.

Unfortunately for KU, that wasn't the only one.

Too many bad possessions on both ends of the court in an uninspired second half signaled KU's doom at the hands of the Longhorns. A couple of possessions involving Rush told the story: a potential defensive rebound that banged off Rush's head and went out of bounds, and a game-tying three-point attempt by the 6-foot-6 Rush that was blocked by 5-11 A.J. Abrams. KU lost its second game of the season by losing in rebounds and hustle points. The Jayhawks led by four points at the half and held a 23-13 rebounding advantage, but Texas finished the game leading in rebounds 36-35.

"We couldn't get our hands on balls," forward Darrell Arthur said, "couldn't grab them. The balls were flying out of bounds. One came off Brandon's head."

In the first half, 13 second-chance points and 24 points in the paint indicated that KU was ready to stake its claim in the conference race. After 20 minutes, the Jayhawks led, 42-38.

Of course, it was easy for the Jayhawks to dominate the Longhorns inside when forward Damion James played only 3 minutes in the first half because of foul

trouble. Self knew that James' return in the second half would play a role, and he figured that Texas coach Rick Barnes would challenge his players to rebound more strongly.

"We talked about that at halftime," Self said, "and our guys did not respond to their aggressiveness. Our guards did a poor job of blocking out in the second half."

James ended up being the key for the Longhorns, who won despite a horrid shooting night from star guard D.J. Augustin. James played all 20 minutes in

the second half, grabbed 13 rebounds and had 12 points.

"Damion had a chance to sit on that bench the first half and boil a little bit because he wants to be out there," Self said. "He came out and kicked our butts in the second half."

Final score
Texas **72**
Kansas...................................69

With Connor Atchley's arms raised high above him, Darrell Arthur worked to shoot the ball.

Feb. 16, 2008

Colorado Buffaloes

Allen Fieldhouse

Old School

For one day, it wasn't about them. Sure, the 2007-2008 Kansas Jayhawks wore blue retro jerseys honoring the 1988 national championship team. Sure, they had a coaching legend spying on their practices. And sure, they blew out Colorado.

But it wasn't about them. This weekend, it was about 230 former KU players, coaches and managers who were in town for a celebration of 110 years of Jayhawk basketball. They came back, great ones and not-so-great ones, for a chance to walk up Naismith Drive on a winter day and relive the past.

Inside Allen Fieldhouse, the old barn that had housed the KU family for 53 years, the current Jayhawks started to get it. Kind of.

"It's hard to get it if you're young," coach Bill Self said. "What will this mean 20 years from now when you come back? We talked a lot today about how cool this is."

Cool. That's the way Mario Chalmers felt when he put on the blue uniforms with the crimson, white and yellow trim, the same look that KU sported the night of April 4, 1988, in Kansas City.

"I love these jerseys," Chalmers said. "I wish we'd keep them and keep playing in them. It's a different look. Old school. I like old school."

The south end of the arena was packed with old-school men who marveled at the Jayhawks' defense of Colorado guard Richard Roby. The Buffaloes' leading scorer was held to only two points and one-of-11 shooting. Kansas held the Buffaloes to 35 percent shooting and forced 15 turnovers.

The effort began in some intense practices after the loss to Texas. All week, there were signs that this game would be different.

Larry Brown knows all of those principles, of course, but the coach of the '88 championship team didn't get technical with the Jayhawks as he watched their practices. Brown's presence at practice two days earlier had an interesting effect on the KU players.

"We threw it all over the gym," Self said. "I asked them, 'What's wrong? You nervous because he's here?' "

Everyone raised his hand. Brown's stop-in was good preparation for this day, when many more KU legends were in their midst.

Final score

Kansas **69**

Colorado 45

Arms outstretched, Sherron Collins flew past Colorado's Jermyl Jackson-Wilson in the first half.

Feb. 23, 2008

Oklahoma State Cowboys
Stillwater, Okla.

Not a pretty day

With nine seconds left and trailing by a single point, the Kansas Jayhawks still had a chance to win. Against Oklahoma State, KU tried basically the same play that failed in the closing seconds at Texas.

Guard Russell Robinson handed the ball to Mario Chalmers, who dribbled into traffic. He kicked the ball out to Brandon Rush, who fired up a contested three-point shot at the buzzer. He missed. All the Jayhawks had needed was a two.

It wasn't pretty. After two losses in three games, the Jayhawks had plenty to ponder.

For one thing, what if Rush could play two halves? Rush went scoreless in the first half, missing all five of his shots, and KU fell apart offensively with 14 turnovers. In the second, Rush went against his passive nature and continued to shoot. He made five of 11 and helped KU fight its way back into the game with 12 points. But it wasn't enough.

Rush's second-half resurgence didn't register with coach Bill Self.

"He had a terrible day," Self said.

For another, what if Darrell Arthur could stay out of foul trouble? Considered the Jayhawks' most talented offensive weapon, the sophomore forward played 17 minutes, scoring six points on one-of-three shooting.

"One of these days," Self said, "we're going to get a consistent 27 to 30 minutes from him."

Arthur, who had spent much time on the bench in Big 12 play, was called for a technical foul with 15 minutes left in the first half that was his second personal. He fouled out at the 6-minute mark while hedging on a screen 22 feet from the basket.

"I couldn't get in any flow of the game," Arthur said.

Meanwhile, Sherron Collins' bruised right knee limited him to 11 minutes.

"He practiced 15 minutes yesterday," Self said. "Obviously, he's a shadow of what he can be."

Finally, what if the Jayhawks had someone like Oklahoma State's Byron Eaton, a player with free rein to dominate? Eaton willed the Cowboys, who had lost 12 games this season, to their improbable victory. All 11,978 fans at Gallagher-Iba Arena knew Eaton was going to drive each time down the floor and make something happen. He finished with 26 points and made 16 of 18 free throws.

Eaton "was the man of the game," forward Darnell Jackson said. "He got it in his mind that he was going to take over the game, and that's what he did."

Rush tried to do the same for Kansas, but it turned out to be too late.

With Oklahoma State's Marcus Dove defending, Darrell Arthur put up a first-half shot

Final score
Oklahoma State **61**
Kansas 60

Late in the game, a worried Kansas bench watched things play out on court.

Violence took a toll

Three days before the Jayhawks' loss to Oklahoma State, Darnell Jackson and Rodrick Stewart lost cousins in shooting incidents hundreds of miles apart.

Jackson's cousin, 19-year-old Kascey Corie McClellan, died of gunshot wounds suffered the week before at an Oklahoma City nightclub. Stewart's cousin, Allen Stewart, 21, was shot to death in Seattle.

It was no wonder that coach Bill Self thought his team was distracted in its game against Oklahoma State.

"It's not the players' fault that they're distracted," Self said. "We had two murders this week with immediate family, and I've never coached that before. I don't know the coaching manual on that."

For Jackson, McClellan's death was the latest catastrophe to befall his family. Jackson's grandmother, Evon, was killed in a 2005 traffic accident and his uncle was beaten to death with a hammer. McClellan is the second cousin of Jackson's who has been shot to death.

Bull Stewart, Rodrick's father, said Allen Stewart was sitting at a stoplight alone when a man pulled up next to his car and opened fire. The Stewart family had adopted Allen when he was a sixth-grader. His mother had been in prison since he was 4 years old and his father was absent, so the Stewarts made him their sixth child.

J. Brady McCollough

Defended tightly by Oklahoma State's Martavius Adams, Mario Chalmers looked to pass the ball to another Jayhawk.

Once again, a victory over the Jayhawks stirred the home team's fans to an on-court celebration, this time in Stillwater.

His bench a patch of blue in a sea of Cowboy orange, Bill Self exhorted his team.

A day later, a pivotal soul-baring

About 3 p.m. on Feb. 24, the entire KU team pushed open the doors of Henry T's. Situated at 6th Street and Kasold on the west side of Lawrence, the restaurant is far removed from the peering eyes of campus or Massachusetts Street, where the Jayhawks would undoubtedly have been hounded if seen together as a team.

Less than a day had passed since they had lost their third game of the season, 61-60 to Oklahoma State. Once 20-0, Kansas suddenly was 24-3 and appeared to be playing its way out of the Big 12 regular-season title race and a high NCAA Tournament seed.

According to KU guard Sherron Collins, the Jayhawks had some chemistry problems, and some things needed to be said.

"Everyone got their feelings out," Collins said, "and no feelings were hurt. Everyone understood it was for the good of the team. Once we got over that, people started listening to each other and didn't take things the wrong way."

The Jayhawks would never lose again. "We figured we had to do

something," KU guard Russell Robinson said. "We wanted it to be an open, relaxed environment, not intense."

Robinson was there as a freshman when the coaches called a meeting in a Philadelphia hotel room after a bad loss to Villanova. That one wasn't much fun. He was also there last season when the Jayhawks met without coaches after barely beating Ball State in Las Vegas. A day later, KU knocked off No. 1 Florida. Both of those meetings were more animated than what Robinson wanted for his 24-3 Kansas team.

So Robinson picked at a shrimp basket and talked to the Jayhawks about energy. The seniors, with their goal of winning four Big 12 regular-season titles slipping away, did most of the talking. Robinson, Darnell Jackson and Jeremy Case led the way, but even Kaun jumped in.

"We needed a lot more energy," Kaun said. "Every day in practice, it should become a habit. It was on and off. We needed to change it where it's every time."

Feb. 27, 2008

Iowa State Cyclones
Ames, Iowa

Picking back up

Was this the night the Kansas Jayhawks became a team again?

"When you're 24-3, you shouldn't be able to say that the ship needs righting," coach Bill Self said. "But our players all know that it did. And we felt it, too."

On this night, on the road against Iowa State, KU played a dominant first half and took a 36-23 lead to the locker room. The Cyclones pushed KU with a 7-0 run beginning the second half, but the Jayhawks pushed back harder. They started an 8-0 run that turned into 21-5. Down 57-35, Iowa State pushed again with an 11-0 run. But Kansas didn't let the Cyclones any closer than nine and won the game.

"This was big, but I don't think we're back where we were," Self said. "I don't think you go from playing poorly to playing great consistently. It's a process. And it was a great start."

By "where we were," Self meant Jan. 30. That morning the Jayhawks woke up an undefeated team, ranked second in the country. Was there any team on KU's schedule capable of beating them? As it turned out, Kansas met that team later that night. Kansas State beat up KU in Bramlage Coliseum and rocked the Jayhawks' cozy world.

"It was a big slap in the mouth to us," Darrell Arthur said. "Ever since we lost to K-State, we've been playing (uphill). We're starting to pick it up now."

The Jayhawks got 18 points and 10 rebounds from Arthur, his fourth double-double of the season. The Cyclones elected not to double-team Arthur, who took 18 high-percentage shots and made nine of them.

Arthur makes everyone around him confident when he's on the floor and not hampered by fouls. That's why Self's first priority in trying to right the ship was to get the ball to Arthur. Russell Robinson and Mario Chalmers both told Arthur

Darnell Jackson went high over Iowa State's Jiri Hubalek for a rebound.

before the game that he was going to have a big night.

Since the K-State game, the Jayhawks had made less than 30 percent of their three-point attempts. For the last few weeks, Rush said, the guards had shot baskets for an extra 15 minutes after practice. That started to pay off in Ames, when KU made seven of 11 threes, its best percentage (63.6 percent) of the season.

In addition, against Iowa State "we showed some toughness," guard Russell Robinson said. "They made some runs. You can't control that all the time. We were able to turn it around."

Toughness is something all the Jayhawks would agree has been lacking in KU's recent slide. Most teams went through their growing pains in the season's first three months, getting losses out of the way early. It was February before Kansas had to question itself.

"We're a tougher team by far because we understand now that we can be beat," Sherron Collins said.

Final score
Kansas **75**
Iowa State 64

March 1, 2008

Kansas State Wildcats

Allen Fieldhouse

Payback time

Brandon Rush had this to say after the rematch of his Jayhawks with Kansas State:

"Beasley was beastly."

Michael Beasley, Kansas State's 6-foot-9 man-child, scored 39 points and grabbed 11 rebounds. That surprised absolutely no one.

But what Rush did was much more relevant. He scored 21 points in leading another balanced Jayhawks' effort to a victory over their in-state rival. His aggressiveness in taking open shots helped sixth-ranked KU pull even with Texas in the Big 12 standings. Rush hit five of nine three-pointers.

"He was terrific offensively," coach Bill Self said.

KU's guards, fueled by a loud-and-proud home crowd, hounded the Wildcats for 10 steals and 14 turnovers in the first half.

It also helped that Beasley and fellow freshman forward Bill Walker spent a large portion of the first half on the bench with foul trouble. Beasley picked up his second foul at the 17-minute, 55-second mark and would play only 12 of the first 20 minutes. Walker, who finished with a quiet nine points, picked up three at the 10-minute mark and played just 19 minutes in the game.

Meanwhile, K-State freshman guard Jacob Pullen, who scored 20 points against KU in the game in Manhattan, finished this game with only three, committing three turnovers along the way.

So there the Jayhawks were, playing their most inspired ball of the season heading into halftime. But what would Rush do? He said that he'd heard he was shut down by K-State's Dominique Sutton in the second half in Manhattan.

"I had a point to prove," Rush said. And he did.

In the first half, Rush was the offensive leader with 13 points. The Jayhawks took a 41-29 lead to halftime after leading by as much as 32-11 early. Rush scored eight more points in a second half that turned out to be largely meaningless after KU started on an 11-0 run and built a 52-29 lead.

Beasley kept going at KU, trying to follow through on his bold guarantee that the Wildcats would beat the Jayhawks in Manhattan, Lawrence and Africa. One fan held a sign that said, "Hey Beasley, if you can win here, I'll pay for your safari." The safari would have to wait.

"They came out and punched us in the first half," Beasley said. "They played with a vengeance."

Final score
Kansas **88**
Kansas State 74

With K-State Coach Frank Martin following the play closely, Sherron Collins drove around C Stewart, above, and past Darren Kent, facing page. Below: Players and fans loved how KU ra three-pointers on the 'Cats.

March 3, 2008

Texas Tech Red Raiders

Allen Fieldhouse

For seniors, parting is sweet

It's no wonder the Jayhawks never lose on Senior Night.

Consider Russell Robinson. In an 8-minute stretch against Texas Tech, Robinson looked like the player he thought he'd be as a freshman. A career 40-percent shooter from the field and a 33-percent three-point shooter, Robinson hit all five of his field-goal attempts and all three from beyond the arc, ending with 15 points.

Kansas won its 24th-straight senior sendoff, sending Texas Tech home with an embarrassing defeat. The 58-point margin of victory was KU's largest ever in a conference game. For three seniors – Robinson, Darnell Jackson, Sasha Kaun, Rodrick Stewart and Jeremy Case – this night was the omega. With this game, their careers playing in front of 16,300 fans at Allen Fieldhouse were over.

All five seniors started, and all had their moments. Robinson, the kid-turned-grownup from the Bronx, N.Y., couldn't miss. That was what he'd imagined when he chose to come to Kansas as a cocky scorer from the big city. But coach Bill Self needed Robinson to run the team from the point.

Jackson, KU's other regular senior starter, thought growing up in Oklahoma City that his future would be in football. It was fitting that two of his finest plays Monday came on quarterback-style passes to his teammates for easy layups. Jackson finished with 10 points and nine rebounds.

For Stewart, a career 19.3 percent shooter on threes, his moment came from beyond the arc. He hit both of his three-point attempts. Case has long been considered a lights-out three-point shooter in practice. In a 2-minute span in the second half, he scored nine points on three treys and sent the crowd into a frenzy.

Last, but certainly not least, Kaun scored 10 points and grabbed four rebounds.

Even walk-on Brad Witherspoon, playing in his last home game, was fouled and hit two free throws.

Kansas' youth was served, too. KU freshman Cole Aldrich had 11 points and 11 rebounds in 17 minutes for his first career double-double.

Final score

Kansas **109**
Texas Tech 51

On the seniors' big night, freshmen got into the act, too. Cole Aldrich, facing page, grabbed a rebound and slammed the ball into the basket despite the efforts of Texas Tech's Charlie Burgess, left, and Trevor Cook. Top: Darnell Jackson gave Aldrich an earful. Above: From the bench, Danny Manning gave the Jayhawks a hand.

March 3, 2008

Texas Tech Red Raiders
Allen Fieldhouse

Tech's John Robertson, above, was hounded by Brandon Rush in the first half. Below, Russell Robinson, Rodrick Stewart and Jeremy Case cheered on the underclassmen.

Who's tops?

Who is the Jayhawks' best player?

Coach Bill Self will leave it to others to determine that.

Texas Tech coach Pat Knight was no help.

"Any one of four or five guys," he said.

Guard Russell Robinson, an assist guy, threw this one away:

"Put five names in a hat and pick them."

Scoring is always a good place to start, but through the regular season Kansas player led the team in scoring more than seven times. Darrell Arthur's 13.6 scoring average was among the lowest in the Big 12 for team leaders. It was an occasion if a Kansas player got 20, and that from a team that averaged 82 points a game.

Rush's overall numbers were down, but in the conference season he was the Jayhawks' top scorer and perhaps best overall player. Darnell Jackson ranked with the league's most improved players. Mario Chalmers, besides leading the Big 12 in steals, ranked among the league's top perimeter shooters.

Then there was the player who didn't often start and wouldn't get any votes for all-conference – Sherron Collins.

With each game, Collins grew stronger and looked more like the Jayhawks' leader and conscience. Kansas might have the country's deepest team. When Collins was on the floor, KU grew fangs. No Kansas player went stronger to the basket, and he was willing, sometimes overly eager, to shoot a three.

Something else. With Kansas leading 80-36 against Texas Tech and regulars yukking it up on the bench, Collins stood next to assistant Kurtis Townsend, calling a defense and yelling instruction, his head in a game that was long past interesting.

For a season's worth of work, give Arthur, or Rush, or Chalmers the nod.

But it was apparent that Collins provided the toughness the Jayhawks need.

J. Brady McCollough

On a court strewn with roses in their honor, the families of KU's seniors gathered with the proud players, above. Below: Coach Bill Self sent five seniors back into the game for one last hurrah.

Later, the speeches

Sasha Kaun: "Coming here from another country was really difficult for me. You guys make me feel like I'm at home."

Kaun on his mother, Olga, who was in the stands: "She doesn't understand half of what I say because she doesn't speak much English. I'm pretty sure she's proud of me right now."

Darnell Jackson: "Coach Self, I just want to know that when I leave here, I hope I have a place in your heart and your home. You helped me out a lot. I love you for that."

Russell Robinson to the fans: "Wear your lucky socks, your lucky shirt, whatever you do. Hopefully, if everything goes to plan, we'll be back here in a few weeks having another great speech."

March 8, 2008

Texas A&M Aggies
College Station, Texas

League co-champs

Coach Bill Self had said that Sherron Collins was the player most capable of masking the Jayhawks' flaws. Flaws? You wouldn't know KU had any by the scoreboard. The Jayhawks beat the Aggies handily and claimed a tie with Texas for the Big 12 championship.

Credit the work of Collins, who owned the game from start to finish. In 32 minutes, he had 13 points, seven assists, three steals and no turnovers. And there were flaws to mask. The Jayhawks shot only two of 11 from three-point range. Darrell Arthur and Darnell Jackson played through foul trouble and eventually fouled out.

For Collins, the stress fracture in his left foot, the turned right ankle and the bruised left knee all felt behind him as he played his best-rounded game so far in the season. To nobody's surprise, so did the Jayhawks.

"There was a stretch in the second half where it was Sherron's game," Self said. "He controlled the game. That's something the people that follow us know we haven't had consistently at all this year."

KU's underclassmen led the charge. Arthur had 16 points on eight-of-10 shooting and added nine rebounds. Mario Chalmers also had 16, and he threw in four rebounds and four steals. It was fitting that the younger players helped the seniors become the ninth group in KU history to win four regular-season titles in a row.

All four rings had their own stories behind them:

When the seniors were freshmen, it was Wayne Simien, Aaron Miles and Keith Langford's team that won a share with Oklahoma. When they were sophomores, it was the fresh-faced Julian Wright, Brandon Rush and Chalmers who led KU to a surprising share with Texas. When they were juniors, it truly was everybody who pushed the Jayhawks to an outright Big 12 title. The latest ring was delivered by sophomores Collins and Arthur.

"It's my last one," Robinson said. "You remember the last one the most."

Final score:

Kansas....................................**72**
Texas A&M 55

Sherron Collins raced downcourt against the Aggies.

**Big 12 Tournament
Kansas City, Mo.**

March 14, 2007

Nebraska Cornhuskers
Kansas City, Mo.

Stirring themselves for the post-season

When the Kansas Jayhawks trailed Nebraska by nine points late in the first half, you didn't need to be a player to figure out what was going on.

"We just weren't into it," Brandon Rush said.

Sherron Collins said, "Teams like that, sometimes you're not psyched up to play them."

The Jayhawks had beaten Nebraska twice this year by an average of 28 points. And they would go on to win this game, too, turning it on after coach Bill Self posed a poignant question at the half:

"Do you want to go home, or do you want to advance?" Self asked.

In its first game of the Big 12 Tournament, KU went on a 20-4 run and pushed the Cornhuskers out of their way.

But the Cornhuskers went down fighting, forcing KU into its worst half of the season. The Cornhuskers trapped KU forward Darrell Arthur when he received the ball in the post, forcing him into four early turnovers. They had lengthy, patient possessions on offense, taking the bite out of Kansas' pressure on the perimeter. The Jayhawks couldn't find a rhythm, and it showed.

Kansas went to halftime down by five points, having committed 12 turnovers.

"That was terrible," Darnell Jackson summed up.

Then came the second half. As he walked from the locker room to the court Sherron Collins could tell that the Jayhawks had picked up the right mindset. Collins saw a Kansas fan in the stands, a total stranger, and motioned to him.

"We're gonna be all right," Collins assured him.

Buoyed by chants of "Let's go, Jayhawks!" from the Sprint Center crowd,

Against Ade Dagunduro, Darnell Jackson slammed the ball home in KU's second-half surge, above. Below: After Sherron Collins received a technical foul for his remarks to the player who fouled him, Mario Chalmers pulled Collins aside for a few words.

the Jayhawks started the second half on a 10-2 run, taking a 32-29 lead. Kansas slowly built its lead from there, and Nebraska began to fade.

KU, as usual, was led by a balanced scoring effort. Collins had 13 points, Mario Chalmers and Jackson had 12, and Sasha Kaun and Rush had nine.

"This was our welcome to the postseason," guard Russell Robinson said.

Once the game was won and relief set in, Self became thankful for the challenge Nebraska gave his team.

"I told our guys, 'We needed this,'" Self said. "We haven't been behind much this year."

Final score
Kansas 64
Nebraska 54

Mario Chalmers and Sherron Collins tried to wrestle the ball from the grasp of Nebraska's Jay-R Strowbridge in the first half, above. Despite the best efforts of Aleks Maric, left, Collins managed to put up this shot and make it while falling.

The Aggies' Bryan Davis worked to get off a shot against Sasha Kaun and Brandon Rush.

March 15, 2007

Texas A&M Aggies *Kansas City, Mo.*

The hot hand

In the semifinal round of the Big 12 tournament, Kansas escaped a valiant effort by Texas A&M, holding on for a six-point victory and setting up the game everyone expected to see: Regular-season co-champions Kansas and Texas in the tournament final.

Rush poured in a career-high 28 points, making nine of 13 attempts. He made five of eight three-pointers and five of five from the free-throw line.

"He had a great look about him, didn't he?" Coach Bill Self said. "Brandon was as good as I've seen him in the last three years."

Sometimes, Rush explained, the ball just goes in the hole. There wasn't some

magical difference that he could point to.

"I was on fire," he said. "I was demanding the ball, and everyone was looking for me because I had the hot hand."

The Jayhawks needed Rush. Sherron Collins got off to a slow start, and Mario Chalmers was hampered by a strained tendon in his knee in the second half. Darrell Arthur struggled through his second straight subpar performance, scoring only seven points.

Rush had eight points in the first half and KU built a 34-26 lead. But the Aggies answered – as they would do all day – going on an 8-0 run at the end of the half. The scoreboard read 34-34, and Texas

A&M coach Mark Turgeon, a former KU player, pumped his fist as he left the floor. Nobody could have imagined what Rush had in store.

Playing in front of a hometown crowd that included his mother, grandmother, father and AAU coach, Rush scored 20 more points in the second half.

As Self saw Rush heating up, he started calling plays to get Rush free.

"When the man is hot," Arthur said, "we just keep going to him."

Final score

Kansas....................................**77**

Texas A&M 71

The Aggies' Chinemelu Elonu watched as Cole Aldrich dunked in the first half, left. Mario Chalmers did his own dunking, above.

Kansas' dance squad, mascot and cheerleaders urged on the Jayhawks, left, while former Jayhawk player Mark Turgeon, above, shouted support for the team he coaches, Texas A&M.

Darrell Arthur grabbed one of his nine rebounds over D. J. Augustin of Texas as Darnell Jackson helped.

March 16, 2007

Texas Longhorns
Kansas City, Mo.

Cool Hand Mario

Mario Chalmers let his Kansas teammates get first dibs with the scissors, cutting down the net. Instead of taking the lead as he had all day, Chalmers soaked up the moment from the back of the line.

Coach Bill Self walked up to Chalmers and put his arm around him. Self, his red tie loosened after a thrilling victory over Texas, shook his head and smiled.

"How was that?" Self said.

"Great," Chalmers replied.

Chalmers is not a man of many words, and he did not need to embellish. His career-high 30 points in yet another big-game performance for the Jayhawks said enough.

Chalmers glanced at his right hand, the one that sent eight three-pointers through those same strips of nylon that his teammates were now wearing under their caps.

"I think it's cooled off now," he said.

That was the question all afternoon as the Big 12 regular-season co-champions battled: Whose right hand would cool off first? Chalmers' or Texas guard D.J. Augustin's? Chalmers hit five of six three-pointers in the first half for 17 points, while Augustin hit all four of his attempts for 18 points. The Longhorns led 46-45 after a first half that 19,047 fans in Kansas City wouldn't soon forget.

The Jayhawks shot nine of 15 from three, and Texas hit eight of 11.

"It was humbling," Self said, "sitting on the sideline and watching the guys play. There were some hard-rocking guys out there today. That was some high-level stuff, probably as high level as I've ever been a part of when you have that many great shot-makers making plays on both sides."

Games like Sunday's are the ones

Chalmers, a native of Anchorage, Alaska, lives for. Augustin was talking with the Kansas players throughout the game, and Chalmers talked right back to him.

Who would back up the talk? Luckily for Chalmers, he had Russell Robinson on his side. Augustin would go zero of nine from the field in the second half. Maybe it was Robinson's defense. Maybe it was the fact that Augustin never left the floor and got tired. Or maybe the shots just weren't falling. While Augustin added only two points for 20 total, Chalmers was just getting started.

With Texas leading 49-47 early in the second half, Chalmers scored Kansas' next eight points. Kansas led 55-52. Chalmers' biggest shot came with KU up by one with 1:52 left, when he nailed his eighth three and put the Jayhawks ahead 75-71. Meanwhile, the Jayhawks won the rebound battle with the Longhorns, 42-10. Texas outrebounded them 23-12 in the second half in Austin.

When it was over, Chalmers tossed the ball into the air. Soon, he'd be the last Kansas player to snip away a piece of the net. After Self climbed the ladder and finished the job, the Jayhawks gathered together one last time.

"One. Two. Three. National champs!" they chanted.

"We started out saying, 'Big 12 regular-season champs,' then we won that," Chalmers explained. "Then we said, 'Big 12 tournament champs,' and we won that. Now, we're moving on to 'National champs,' and we're going to try to win that, too."

Final score
Kansas **84**
Texas 74

His jaw dropping, Coach Bill Self watched Brandon Rush try to block a shot by the Longhorns' Justin Mason.

Dexter Pittman of Texas and Sasha Kaun went after a first-half rebound.

This team can go deep

The Kansas Jayhawks are a lot like the Big 12 tournament at the Sprint Center, nearly impossible to dislike in March.

Sure, Bill Self's Jayhawks have done this before – capped the conference season by throttling Texas in the championship game – and bailed on the Big Dance before the music really started jamming. No one will forget Bucknell and Bradley. The loss to UCLA in the Elite Eight still stings.

This time it feels different, doesn't it? These Jayhawks have experienced depth, a handful of NBA players and a collective chemistry that previous Self editions lacked. They also have a sense of urgency.

"This is the year," said Brandon Rush, the tournament's MVP. "This is the year we've got to do it. We've got five seniors leaving. Some people might be leaving early. We've got to make it happen. We're not ever going to have a team like this again."

You can call that pressure. Or you can call it an acceptance of KU's reality. Whatever it is, it's Bill Self's job to turn it into motivation that drives the Jayhawks on a postseason winning streak.

The Jayhawks are no Final Four locks, but you have to like their chances – if they can play somewhere near the level they displayed against Texas.

It's hard to imagine the Jayhawks screwing this up. It's unfair to judge a coach or a program by one or even two tournament disappointments. I'm always of the opinion that regular-season success means more than postseason success. But this time, I'll be disappointed if Kansas doesn't win four. Self has too many pieces to work with. He won't see a team with equal talent until the Final Four.

Yeah, the Jayhawks should be feeling some pressure right now. They can handle it.

Jason Whitlock

NCAA Tournament

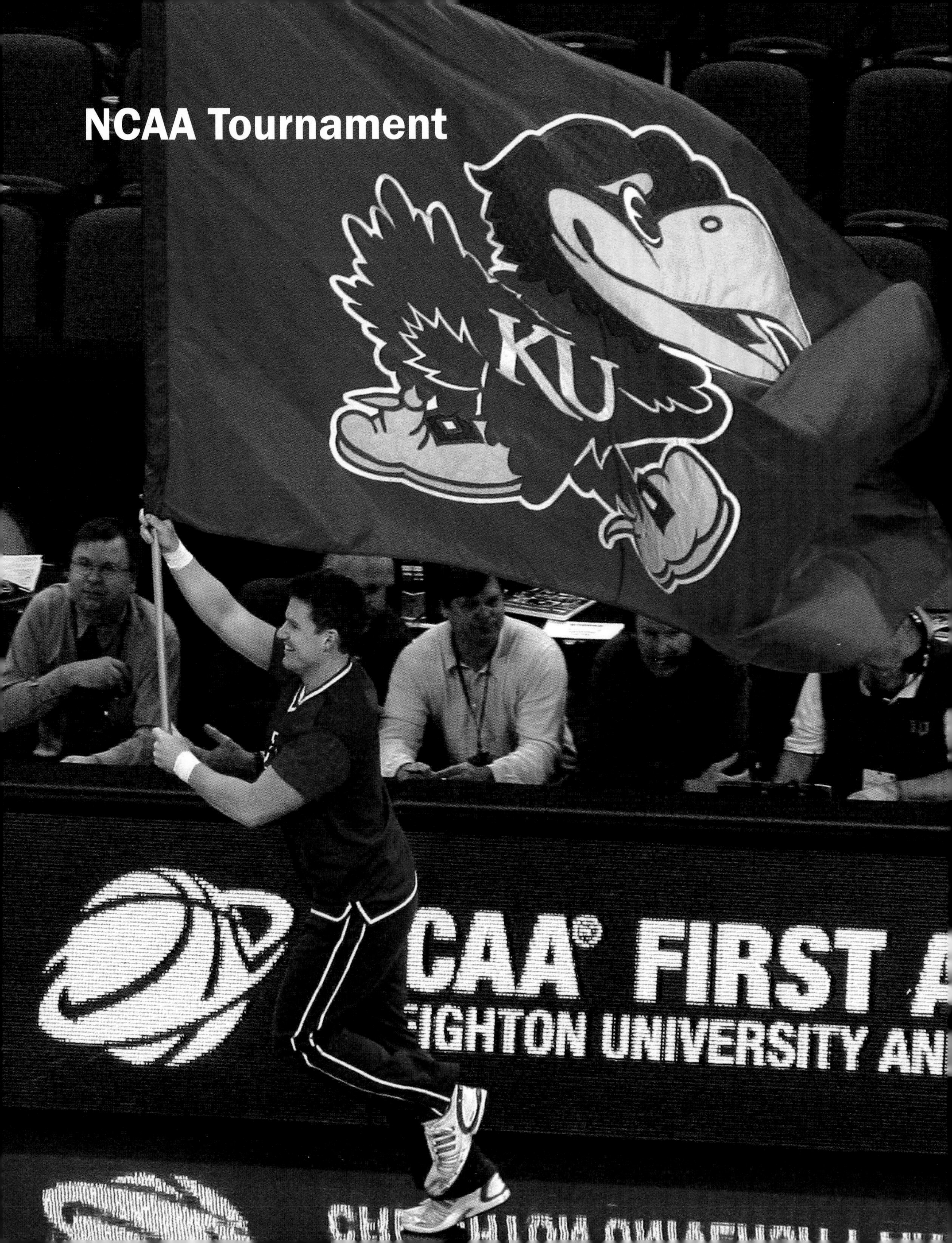

It's OK, KU can look ahead

Fate, I believe, is Kansas' best weapon this NCAA Tournament season. The Jayhawks are meant to play the North Carolina Tar Heels in the semifinals of the Final Four. There is not one doubt in my mind that we will see Bill Self and Roy Williams square off in San Antonio.

It's meant to be.

A Self vs. Williams battle in the Final Four would be just as hyped, anticipated and bitter as the football and basketball wars among Kansas, Kansas State and Missouri that occupied us in the fall and winter.

Kansas-North Carolina would be a terrific dessert. It's going to happen.

Five years after Roy's departure, Self and Williams have done exactly what they were hired to do at Kansas and Carolina. They rebuilt elite programs and assembled teams with lots of future NBA talent and likable players. OK, Roy won a national championship at Carolina with Matt Doherty's players. So it's really fair to say that this is the best UNC team Williams has recruited and coached. The same can be said for Self.

I don't think you'll get much argument if you claim that Kansas and North Carolina are the two most talented teams in college basketball.

Tyler Hansbrough is a better college player than any player on KU's roster. But Kansas could offset UNC's Hansbrough advantage with superior depth and guard play.

There's no legitimate way to predict a winner. The teams are too evenly matched. The game would be decided by officiating and Darrell Arthur's ability to avoid foul trouble. As a sports fan and writer, Kansas-Carolina would be the perfect way to finish a dream college season.

Jason Whitlock
(*Kansas City Star, March 20, 2008*)

March 20, 2008

Portland State Vikings
Omaha, Neb.

The A game

They say the key to winning in March is for each player to know his role. The Kansas Jayhawks just happened to wait until March to define theirs, beginning NCAA tournament play with a blowout of Portland State.

"Everybody understands their role now," Sherron Collins said, "and by this time, if you don't understand your role, you probably won't have a clue and you won't make it that far in the tournament."

KU's big names continued to play big. Brandon Rush had 18 points, Darrell Arthur had 17 – and only two fouls – and Mario Chalmers had 16.

Just as important to the Jayhawks was the supporting cast. Point guard Russell Robinson didn't take a shot the entire first half, focusing on setting the pace and pressuring Jeremiah Dominguez, the Vikings' jitterbug guard. Darnell Jackson and Sasha Kaun did the dirty work inside and threw down a couple of monster dunks. Sherron Collins bowled into the lane for a team-high five assists.

The top-seeded Jayhawks played like a team with a clue for one half, and that was more than enough to move into the second round. Kansas built a 49-26 halftime lead over the Vikings by shooting 64.3 percent from the field and hitting eight of 13 three-point attempts.

Any thought of KU becoming the first No. 1 seed to lose to a No.16 seed was in flames after 5 minutes, when the Jayhawks led 13-3 and had three dunks in 4 minutes.

"When guys came out hot, the jitters got out pretty quick," said Arthur, who hit his first four shots. "We brought our A-game offensively."

All season, the Jayhawks have sworn by their balance, the notion that it could be any of them leading the team in scoring on any given night. KU still had balance, but its players weren't tripping over each other any longer. It seemed more natural now with Rush, Arthur and Chalmers taking most of the shots.

"Hey, shooters shoot it, rebounders rebound it, screeners screen it, and passers pass it," Self said.

The Jayhawks appeared to have settled on a seven-man rotation as a base, with Cole Aldrich and Rodrick Stewart playing in spells when the game was tight. Those seven have never felt so right together.

Darrell Arthur finished one dunk, above, and got another one after a backdoor cut, facing page.

"The main thing all season is to prepare for these six games, for this tournament," Robinson said. "This is the part of the season when everyone has to be clicking on all cylinders."

Final score
Kansas **85**
Portland State 61

March 22, 2008

Nevada-Las Vegas Runnin' Rebels
Omaha, Neb.

The guards take over

Yes, the Kansas Jayhawks had bigger goals than the Sweet 16. And no, they didn't get to cut down any nets on this night. Still, they felt relieved to walk off the Qwest Center floor with a hard-fought victory over No. 8 seed Nevada-Las Vegas.

"The first weekend is when the upsets happen," senior Jeremy Case said, "when the bad things happen."

KU's juniors and seniors knew that from experience. The first weekend of the NCAA Tournament is always about survival. Style points don't matter, and for the first 30 minutes, the Jayhawks were certainly lacking in style. They had spent all game trying to assert their inside dominance over the smaller Runnin' Rebels, who didn't start a player bigger than 6 feet, 7 inches.

But Kansas' big men found themselves in foul trouble, and many empty possessions came from Coach Bill Self's high-low offense. Surprisingly, UNLV had more offensive rebounds than Kansas, 9-7, and took 15 more free throws than the Jayhawks.

So what would give? Despite pregame talk about how the contest would center on KU's post players, it would be up to the guards.

At the 10:55 mark, with KU up 50-42, Self put in a lineup with KU's top four guards and Sasha Kaun. The offensive set is called "five man," and it relies on Kaun to free the guards, who are spread along the perimeter. The Jayhawks went on a 10-2 run and suddenly built a 60-44 lead.

"That definitely helped us out a lot," KU guard Russell Robinson said. "We haven't had to go to the four-guard offense in a while. It worked for us today."

And it wasn't all Brandon Rush and Mario Chalmers this time. Robinson had 10 second-half points and finished with 13, and Sherron Collins had 10 points after a scoreless first half. Rush and Chalmers finished with 12 and 17 points, respectively.

Thanks to the burst of energy from the guard-heavy lineup, the Jayhawks overcame a terrific performance from UNLV guard Wink Adams, who willed himself to 25 points by going 15 of 17 from the free-throw line.

The Runnin' Rebels were able to hang with KU because they withstood the Jayhawks' initial push, the part of the first half when the Jayhawks try to overwhelm the opponent with high-flying dunks and pressure defense. KU went on a 13-3 run and led 13-6, and Darrell Arthur, Chalmers and Kaun all dunked emphatically.

But UNLV answered back, unlike KU's first-round opponent, Portland State. The Runnin' Rebels took an 18-17 lead at the 7:48 mark.

"They tried to come out and punk us," Chalmers said, "but we didn't back down. We kept fighting with them."

The Runnin' Rebels impressed KU with their effort, but it's hard to upset a No. 1 seed when you shoot 26.7 percent from the field and make just 12 field goals.

Kansas never panicked, even when things weren't coming easy.

"You can't get scared at this point," Robinson said, "but we were a little concerned. We stuck to our game plan and kept putting it on them."

KU could pack its bags for the Sweet 16 in Detroit, but in the Kansas locker room after the game, there wasn't much celebration.

"We're happy to be at the Sweet 16, but we're supposed to be there," Case said. "We're happy, but we're not satisfied."

Final score
Kansas **75**
UNLV 56

Sasha Kaun went up for a shot, guarded closely by UNLV defenders.

Darnell Jackson snagged a rebound from UNLV's Matt Shaw.

Time to rest

Self hoped that an extra day off – in the upcoming regionals, KU was scheduled to play on a Friday instead of a Thursday – would help point guard Sherron Collins recover from a bruised left knee he suffered in practice before the Portland State game. Collins bumped the same knee that hobbled him in last year's Elite Eight loss to UCLA. Earlier this season, Collins bruised his right knee. Just as that began to heal, he bruised the left one again. Collins played through it against UNLV, scoring 10 points.

J. Brady McCollough

Darrell Arthur struck with a two-handed dunk.

March 28, 2008

Villanova Wildcats
Detroit

Alley-oop, again

With three NCAA Tournament games in the books, the Kansas Jayhawks might have wondered: Could it really be this easy?

After this, an annihilation of No. 12 seed Villanova, the Jayhawks stood one win from sacred basketball ground and still had not experienced a tense moment in the Big Dance.

"Even though we're winning by a lot," guard Russell Robinson said, "the games are a lot tougher than they look."

Certainly, they hadn't looked tough. Maybe Kansas was just that good.

Kansas sent a message early against Villanova, jumping out to a 24-10 lead and never letting the Wildcats closer than seven. The tournament had other upsets, but there would be none this game.

"We've played good teams," guard Sherron Collins said. "We've just been able to jump out on them and get leads and keep the lead on them."

In what was quickly becoming a trend in March, the Jayhawks again were led by their guard play. Robinson had 13 points in the first 9 minutes and finished with 15. But his most vital contribution was his defense against Villanova's Scottie Reynolds, who had only 11 points after averaging 23 points in the Wildcats' two previous tournament games.

KU coach Bill Self, who took an 0-4 record into his fifth Elite Eight game, said Robinson was the key for Kansas on Friday. But he wasn't alone. Brandon Rush led KU with 16 points, and Chalmers had 14.

The Wildcats were never truly a threat to KU, but if the game had a turning point, it was late in the first half when Villanova used an 8-0 run to pull within 28-21. The Wildcats appeared to have some life, but Chalmers scored eight consecutive points, got KU back on track and helped the Jayhawks take a 41-22 lead into the locker room.

KU's three guards – Chalmers, Robinson and Rush – combined for 32 points, while Reynolds could only muster six for the Wildcats in the first half.

Once again, the Jayhawks spent a tournament game putting on a clinic on how to execute an alley-oop. Four different players – Darnell Jackson, Sasha Kaun, Darrell Arthur and Rush – had the pleasure of finishing those plays.

Two days later, KU would go for its 11th consecutive victory and a trip to San Antonio against No. 10 seed Davidson, which upset No. 3 seed Wisconsin.

Final score
Kansas **72**
Villanova 57

Alley-oops all, by Darnell Jackson, above, and Sasha Kaun, left.

From right, Jeremy Case, Russell Robinson and Sasha Kaun swatted at the ball as Villanova's Scottie Reynolds drove the lane.

They need his grit

Villanova coach Jay Wright said something interesting this week. He was asked to describe the thing that separates the big-city, New York point guards from the rest. He said there was one thing: New York guards seem to have this inner sense about when they need to step out of their character and make something happen.

In this case, Kansas guard Russell Robinson, who grew up (of course) on the asphalt courts of New York, seemed to understand that he needed to score early and often. He did. The odd part was that the key moments in the game came early. Robinson poured in 13 points in the first 8 minutes of the game Friday night. He made three three-pointers. He controlled the game.

And when his scoring flurry ended, Kansas led Villanova by 14 points, and the game, in all significant ways, was over. In fact, you kind of wish the game would have ended there. What followed was like 32 minutes of credits rolling after a movie.

"I didn't think in the second half, we had much rhythm," Self would say.

And that was an understatement. The game turned into a sumo wrestling match, with both teams just leaning on each other for the last 30 minutes. Kansas did win by 15. But the atmosphere was a dead zone. The crowd in the dome yawned and headed for home.

Then, it's the tournament so only three words matter: Survive and advance. Those first 9 minutes were the whole ballgame, and they remind you just how important Robinson was to this Jayhawks team.

It's easy to overlook him. He's not a big NBA prospect like Darrell Arthur, and he can't shoot the ball anything like Brandon Rush, and he can't take over on both sides of the floor with his athletic ability and skill like Mario Chalmers, and he can't just change the game like Sherron Collins.

And still ... you get the sense that for the Jayhawks to do what they want to do, Robinson would be key. He's the senior point guard. You know how much those guys matter in March. He's the Jayhawks best on-the-ball defender – he was the guy most responsible for shutting down Villanova's big scorer, Scottie Reynolds. He's the guy – especially with Collins hurting – who will be asked to control the tempo, and calm teammates down when things go bad, and fire everyone up when their energy level drops.

And I just get the sense that he's the one who – Wright is right – will need to step out of character just when the Jayhawks need it most. This Jayhawks team is good. Really good. They can win so many different ways that you sometimes sense they spend the first few minutes of the game deciding which way to do it.

They have not been tested yet in the tournament. Villanova tried to muddy up the game – and the Wildcats managed that, especially in the second half – but Kansas simply moved the ball around too well and got too many easy shots to get beat by a team that can't score. Villanova on its best night should not beat Kansas.

Davidson could provide a challenge Sunday simply because the Wildcats must feel like a team of destiny, and they have the player of the tournament – one of the great players of any tournament – Stephen Curry. Still Kansas is bigger, stronger, faster. They're called Cinderellas because, eventually, midnight strikes.

Joe Posnanski

This was going to be it – the shot that determined the winner. Hot shooter Stephen Curry, far right, was too closely guarded so he passed it to Jason Richards for the final attempt, which Richards launched from behind the three-point arc...

For Coach Bill Self, who had never made the semi-finals of the NCAA tournament, the victory over Davidson removed a massive emotional weight.

March 30, 2008

Davidson Wildcats
Detroit

Tick...tick...tick

Sixteen seconds. That's what the Kansas Jayhawks could tell their children and grandchildren about. One possession frozen in time.

The entire country was watching, rooting against them. That's how the story would start.

Davidson's Stephen Curry had been making improbable shots the whole tournament, and how was this for improbable? If he hit another three-pointer, the No. 10 seed Davidson Wildcats – tiny Davidson College – would beat the No. 1 seed Kansas Jayhawks and go to the Final Four.

Leading by two points, coach Bill

Self told his players not to let Curry shoot a three under any circumstances. Curry received the in-bounds pass, and Russell Robinson stayed with him the whole way. Curry pump-faked, but there was no opening.

Three seconds left. Still nothing. He passed to Jason Richards.

Two seconds. Richards heaved a long three with Brandon Rush flying at him.

One second. They all turned and looked.

The ball banged harmlessly off the backboard as the red light flashed. Kansas had won.

"Quickest 16 seconds ever," Robinson would say. Robinson dashed to half court,

...but the shot clanked off to the left of the hoop. The backboard lit up, signaling that time had expired. Only then could the Jayhawks celebrate.

straight into the waiting arms of fellow senior Jeremy Case, who had run up from the Kansas bench. For Robinson and Case, the story ended right there. It's the one about how a gritty group of seniors and the coach who recruited them finally arrived at the place they always wanted to go, the Final Four.

"San Antonio," senior Darnell Jackson said. "That's what's going through everybody's mind. Just how scary it was, when Davidson got that last shot off.

"You can see how it was out there. You never know how it's going to go in a game. It can go downhill and uphill. For us it went uphill."

KU's seniors – except for Case, who was recruited by Williams – formed Self's first recruiting class. In three years, they had never ended their season on a high note. And that's putting it lightly. First, it was Bucknell. Then, it was Bradley. Both were in the first round. In 2007, it was UCLA in the Elite Eight, and that may have hurt the most.

Davidson came to Ford Field for this game with the full intention of adding its name to the list. The Wildcats of the Southern Conference hounded the Jayhawks defensively from the tip. The score was 9-9 after 10 minutes. Meanwhile, Curry started to get going. He hit from everywhere, inside and outside.

"You're thinking, 'Try not to let the crowd get in your head,'" Robinson said. "Every time he hit a shot, it was like Jordan hitting a shot or something. The whole nation was tuning in, and you just didn't want to show any negative emotion."

Coach Bill Self was thinking the same thing. He was on the verge of losing his fifth Elite Eight game, to a school nobody had heard of before this tournament, but he told his guys to stay calm.

"You can't wish it to happen," Self told them. "You gotta make it happen."

His team had trailed Davidson 51-47 with 7 minutes, 13 seconds remaining. Then the Jayhawks went on a 7-0 run. Still, Self had a feeling about how this one would end.

"I knew it would come down to us

Outfitted in caps and T-shirts for the occasion, KU players shouted in glee at making the 2008 Final Four.

being on defense and getting a stop," Self said.

And Kansas played its best defensive possession of the year – possibly the last five years.

"If (Curry) shot it from half court, I would say that's pitiful defense," Self said, "because he's going to make it."

But he didn't even shoot it. Davidson's 16 seconds in the spotlight were up, and it was finally Self's chance to cut down the nets after a regional final – that is, if his Jayhawks would leave him some net to cut.

"Don't cut it all, Cole!" Self yelled to freshman Cole Aldrich.

Self walked up the eight steps on the ladder. It had been quite a climb, trying to win one of these. After he snipped the remaining nylon and pumped his fist, Self grabbed a microphone to address the KU fans.

"See you at the River Walk!" he said.

For Kansas, a new tale had begun. The Jayhawks would play in their first national semifinal since 2003 against North Carolina and former KU coach Roy Williams.

Final score

Kansas **59**
Davidson 57

No. 1 in the Midwest region was KU's seed and the Jayhawks played to it, taking home the trophy from Ford Field in Detroit.

Finally!

Bill Self watched the last shot on both knees. It was that sort of ending. Someone should have passed around a collection plate. Self watched Davidson's Jason Richards catch the ball at the top of the key, shoot it in an off-balance way, and as the clock dropped to 0:00, the ball lofted toward the basket, it looked no good, then good, then not so good again – victory, then defeat, then ....

Then the ball hit the backboard. Bounced away. The buzzer sounded. Kansas beat Davidson 59-57. Bill Self, in his fifth chance, would take a team to the Final Four. Self dropped his head. He slapped the floor with his hand. He walked toward the Davidson bench in a dazed way – like a boxer walking back to his corner after a crushing punch. He hugged his family. He cut down the final strands of the net. He got doused with water in the locker room.

Sometimes breakthroughs don't come with ticker-tape parades. This game had not played at all the way Bill Self had imagined. He expected this Kansas-Davidson game to be close, painfully close. But he did not expect it to be this kind of close. His Jayhawks played scared. Self had not seen that coming. His Jayhawks played as if they were wearing Buick-sized ankle weights.

"Attack the attacker," Davidson coach Bob McKillop had told his players, and the Wildcats came at the Jayhawks, pounded inside with the bigger players, pressed them full court, defended Kansas with gusto. Of course, Self knew that Davidson would do those things; the Wildcats had upset Gonzaga, Georgetown and Wisconsin by doing those things, by attacking the attacker.

No, Self's surprise came when the Jayhawks backed down. They scored one basket in the first 5 minutes of the game. They short-armed shots they had made all year. At one point in the first half, they were so flustered they called two timeouts on the same possession. They looked lifeless – no, they were trying, it was something else. They seemed frozen with stage fright.

Self sat on his stool on the sideline, and his face was flush with disbelief. This was his nightmare. He could take losing. But he could not take his team playing timid basketball.

"What's going on out there?" he screamed more than once.

It was, frankly, hard to tell what was going on. The only thing that was clear was that Kansas did not look at all like Kansas. The Jayhawks' offense – so smooth, so crisp, so lethal so much of the year – seemed to be running in slow motion, as if under strobe lights. The Jayhawks had trouble just getting the ball inbounds. Their fast break was virtually nonexistent. The Jayhawks' alley-oop, a specialty all year, did not oop once the whole first half.

"Go! Go! Go!" Self screamed at his guys, and he made helpful hand gestures, but something was wrong. The Jayhawks would not go. It was strange.

And then again, maybe it was not. Pressure will do strange things to men. The pressure on this Jayhawks team was immense.

First, none of them had ever been to a Final Four. The seniors had lost in the first round twice and they had been beaten down by UCLA in the Elite Eight last year. They knew the score.

Second, they were playing America's darlings, a team that seemed to be touched by magic the whole tournament. Everyone was rooting for Davidson.

Third, this was the last regional final – and the first three No. 1 seeds had already made it into the tournament. If Kansas lost, then the Jayhawks alone would be seen as a No. 1 failure.

And fourth, probably the most important factor, everyone wanted so much to win this game for Self. Nobody wanted to see him go through the suffering of another Elite Eight defeat, especially to a tiny and feisty No. 10 seed like Davidson. Self is a good guy. Everyone likes him. Players respect him. Nobody wanted to see him lose again.

"This game has a different feel to it than a lot of other games," Self would say. "I thought we were loose. I thought everything was great. Warm-ups, everything was great. But ... everyone knows the stakes are so high."

Whatever the reason, the Kansas players were not themselves. But here's one thing that's special about this team that Self has built: These Jayhawks can beat you more than one way.

And although the Jayhawks seemed

to play shell-shocked offense, they still did play ferocious, Bill Self defense. They sent a wave of defenders at Davidson's brilliant guard Stephen Curry, and they managed to do what no other team could do. They wore him down. Curry still scored 25 points and made some breathtaking plays, but he missed six consecutive three-pointers in the final minutes, and he would admit that the defensive deluge did exhaust him.

That's what kept the game close and intense. Maybe that's only justice; Self often talks about how, as a coach, he prefers the slow, grind-it-out kind of games. Well, here it was. Neither team ever led by more than six points. It really was a Self kind of game.

And there would be no easy ways out. With 36.3 seconds left, and Kansas up by two, Self called a timeout and set up a play. If the Jayhawks could just score, they could more or less put away the game. Instead – as they had all game long – Kansas could not get any rhythm on offense, and the play ended with Sherron Collins taking a desperation three-pointer just as the shot clock was about to expire. The ball banged off the side of the rim and ricocheted out of bounds.

That gave Davidson one last chance, one more glass slipper. That's what led to Jason Richards' final shot, the missed three-pointer that Bill Self watched on his knees.

"I just wanted to make sure that I hurried up and shook hands and the officials left the court so they couldn't put any more time back on the clock," Self would say.

Now, Self and Kansas were headed to the Final Four and a whole new kind of pressure. There would be no time to celebrate. It wasn't just that Self was taking a Kansas team to the Final Four and a shot at the national title. No, he would have to prepare his team for North Carolina and Roy Williams and a whole week's worth of stories and ghosts.

Of course, Self wouldn't trade it for anything. He made it. They made it. A reporter asked Self whether he felt as if an 800-pound gorilla had been removed from his shoulder.

"I thought it was 1,200 pounds," the coach replied.

Joe Posnanski

The Final Four

April 5, 2008

North Carolina Tar Heels
San Antonio

Beating Roy

They had heard the comparisons all year. It was the 20th anniversary of 1988, of Danny and the Miracles, and this year's KU team was sure to be really good. But those comparisons, until the Final Four was set, never involved the word underdog.

Yet that's what the Kansas Jayhawks were when they took the floor against the tournament's top seed, North Carolina, and player of the year Tyler Hansbrough. The question was what happened when you gave a team loaded with talent like the Jayhawks an underdog label in the biggest game of their lives?

The answer: A masterpiece.

Kansas beat former KU coach Roy Williams and his Tar Heels in a game so lopsided by the end that Jayhawks coach Bill Self got to empty his bench and play his walk-ons. The underdog role worked in '88 when sixth-seeded KU beat Duke and Oklahoma in the Final Four — and was working again two decades later in the Alamodome on a lesser scale.

"Everyone said we're an underdog," Sherron Collins said, "but we didn't come in thinking we're the underdog. We came in expecting to win, and that's what we did."

Kansas, a shell of itself six days earlier in a two-point win over Davidson, was relaxed and ready to seize the moment in San Antonio.

"Davidson game, it was so much pressure," guard Russell Robinson said. "Coach Self trying to get to his first Final Four. Davidson was the Cinderella of the tournament. All the No. 1 seeds had already made it. In this game, all of that was gone. We got by the tough part. This is the easy part."

The Jayhawks made it look that way most of the night. They would meet fellow No. 1 seed Memphis in the national championship game, their first title bout since 2003, when KU lost to Syracuse.

It would be ridiculous, of course, for the Jayhawks to play the underdog card again. After all, the secret is out: This collection of Kansas players brings it against top competition.

"Last year we came out and played great against Florida," KU sophomore Darrell Arthur said. "This year, we've been wanting to play North Carolina since November. All the guys were pumped to play."

There were hints all week that KU guard Brandon Rush was going to play his best game — the laid-back junior actually snapped at a teammate at practice. Rush saved the rest of his energy for North Carolina, with a game-high 25 points and seven rebounds.

The parallels to KU's 1988 run had been eerie — starting with the Jayhawks' road to the Final Four, which also went through tournament sites in Nebraska and Michigan — and the similarities continued in San Antonio when Rush played the role of Danny Manning. When North Carolina pulled within four at 54-50, Rush scored on a layup. When the Tar Heels cut it to six at 67-61, Rush again went to the hole for two.

"In order for us to win," Rush said, "someone was going to have to step up and make some big plays for us tonight."

Rush's bucket started a 13-0 run for the Jayhawks, the third and most crucial run of the game for both teams.

Kansas won the first 15 minutes by a whopping margin of 40-12. Down the street from the Alamo, KU drew a line in the sand from the opening tip. If Ol' Roy's team was going to beat the school he coached for 15 years, the Tar Heels were going to do it with an elbow in the back and a hand in the face.

The Jayhawks simply wouldn't let them do anything – not until the first 15 minutes were up. North Carolina started

North Carolina's and the country's player of the year, Tyler Hansbrough, put up an off-balance shot against Sasha Kaun, one of the KU big men who guarded him closely all night. Facing page: While Brandon Rush roared in joy, Tar Heel Coach Roy Williams could only watch.

making the shots it was missing and won the next 17 minutes by a score of 41-18. The Tar Heels trailed just 58-53 at the 8-minute mark.

KU won the last eight minutes 26-13, and that was that. They outrebounded the Tar Heels 42-33 and held Hansbrough to 17 points on six-of-13 shooting.

Could they do it once more?

"This is what you live for," Robinson said. "You gotta have faith."

Final score

Kansas..................................	**84**
North Carolina	66

After the game, an ecstatic Coach Bill Self and his team did interviews with CBS television's Jim Nantz and Billy Packer.

Revenge is fabulous

Five years of pain and frustration provoked 15 fabulous minutes.

You can't forget the Fab 15. Not if you love Kansas, loathe the way Roy Williams departed for North Carolina and appreciate beautiful basketball.

The Kansas Jayhawks served Roy Williams revenge steaming hot, blazing to a 28-point advantage to open their Final Four semifinal showdown and settling their emotional divorce from Williams on terms KU fans can live with. It was quite possibly the most impressive 15 minutes of play in the school's storied history.

"It's the best 15 I've ever had anybody play," Kansas coach Bill Self said, "because you're playing against the No. 1 seed on the biggest stage."

Of course, the Jayhawks couldn't sustain their magnificent play Saturday night; they allowed the Tar Heels to rally from a 40-12 deficit to make the second half super competitive for a time.

Carolina's comeback was somewhat predictable. You knew the Jayhawks' shooting would eventually cool. They started the game sinking 16 of their first 23 shots. Kansas was too long for North Carolina on the inside, and Brandon Rush was too hot on the perimeter. Rush scored 15 of his game-high 25 points during the Fab 15. And Kansas' Bermuda Rectangle of big men limited Tyler Hansbrough to a quiet 17-point, nine-rebound night.

But you also knew the Tar Heels would rally because you remembered the reason Kansas fans worshipped Williams for 15 years. Williams-coached teams do not quit. Ever. And the Tar Heels didn't on Saturday, climbing all the way back to within 54-50 midway through the second half.

The Tar Heels matched Kansas' Fab 15 with 15 remarkable minutes of their own, outscoring KU 38-14 at the end of the first half and the beginning of the second.

"As good as we played early, we played about that poorly in the middle," Self said.

But the Jayhawks regrouped and reasserted control of the game. With their outside shooting MIA, the Jayhawks rediscovered their big men — Sasha Kaun,

Cole Aldrich, Darrell Arthur and Darnell Jackson.

No doubt, Kansas' backcourt played brilliantly. Rush, Mario Chalmers and Sherron Collins put up big numbers and scored crucial baskets. But the Jayhawks won on Saturday because of their dominance in the frontcourt.

Kaun, Aldrich, Arthur and Jackson frustrated Hansbrough in the low post. College basketball's player of the year could never find a comfortable rhythm in the paint. He went long stretches without getting a shot. He was not dominant on the boards. The player described as the hardest working in basketball did not appear any more active than Aldrich, Kansas' little-used freshman who collected six rebounds in the first half and finished the contest with a game-high four blocks.

Arthur swatted four, too. Jackson scored 12 points in 17 minutes and hit five of six shots. Kaun rebounded from an ineffective first half and dropped in two baskets after the break. KU's frontcourt spurred the Jayhawks to a 42-33 rebound advantage.

North Carolina simply could not deal with Kansas' size. And the Tar Heels couldn't match Kansas' emotion and physical play.

This game meant more to Kansas.

Jason Whitlock

Darnell Jackson and Darrell Arthur marked their success with a big-man-sized embrace.

That chant

The lasting image happened in the final seconds, when Roy Williams stood on the sideline, and Kansas fans chanted "Rock Chalk." It was the first time as a head basketball coach that Williams heard that chant from the losing bench. There had to be some strange emotions rumbling inside the man.

He would not talk about those emotions afterward. No. He said the things he always said in such moments, after his team had been outplayed and out-toughed in the NCAA Tournament. He said that he apologized to his players for letting them down. He said that he's proud as all get-out. He talked about how he coaches such good kids.

"I wouldn't trade teams because of the character our guys have," Williams said after it ended. And, as usual, he caught himself.

"That's not a slight to Kansas," he said.

The speech was as familiar as Thanksgiving turkey, and yet … it sounded strange to hear it from the other side. Kansas manhandled North Carolina on Saturday. There's no mistaking that. Kansas beat North Carolina 84-66. It was a knockout.

Many had come into Saturday's game expecting to see North Carolina run free, score at will, put up 90 points, maybe 100; the Tar Heels were the first team in years to score 100 points in each of their first two NCAA Tournament games. Kansas, many figured, would get washed away.

Then something happened. Old sportswriters tell a great story about the first time Muhammad Ali — Cassius Clay then — fought against Sonny Liston. Leading up to the fight, everyone portrayed Liston as this blood-thirsty monster who could not be stopped, could not be hurt — people literally were worried that Liston would kill Clay.

Then the two men stepped in the ring for the fight, and a few sportswriters noticed during the pre-fight introductions that Clay was actually bigger than Liston. And they realized they had been duped. And Clay battered Liston into submission.

Same thing here. Outsiders may have

expected North Carolina to score furiously, but just minutes into the game, they also realized that they had been duped. Kansas can play defense with any team in the country. This is what Bill Self has been instilling in Kansas basketball ever since he arrived five years ago. He admires Roy Williams' coaching, but he does not agree with it. He wants his players in their players' faces.

From the start, they were in the faces of those North Carolina players. And they didn't like it. Well, nobody really does, but Williams' teams may like it less.

Sure, Roy Williams said that he tried to warn his players, tried to prepare them. He explained afterward that he had told his players all those things coaches say when facing a great defensive team: Don't take quick shots. Be strong with the ball. Meet the pass. Guards, don't try and dribble between two defenders. Don't dribble in traffic. And so on.

But those are just principles. In the end, it's hard for high-scoring teams to believe that they can be stopped by anybody.

It was pretty clear that was the Tar Heels' whole attitude coming into this game. They came prepared for a track meet and, instead, found themselves in a tough-man contest. They got knocked out early. Kansas led 7-2, then 15-8, then 23-10, then 32-10, then 40-12 — it was incredible, ridiculous, nobody could believe what was happening.

Big leads, like money, youth and weekends, disappear faster than you think — especially against those high-scoring

Roy Williams teams. Who could forget the furious comeback his 1997 Kansas team had against Arizona after trailing by 13 with three and a half minutes to go?

But that comeback, like most furious comebacks, fell short. And Saturday, while North Carolina did manage to cut Kansas' lead to four in the second half, they had nothing left for the finish, and the Jayhawks mercilessly put them away. It might be right to say North Carolina threw a scare into the Jayhawks. But it would not be right to say the game was close.

With about a minute left, Roy Williams heard the "Rock Chalk" chant. Williams would say after the game that he never really thought about playing his old school, not after the game began. That might be true. But it had to be strange for him to hear that familiar chant, the one that ended most of his Kansas victories, the one that had for so many years sounded like a Christmas carol, something that made him feel good.

It definitely felt strange for us to hear him say all those things we had heard him say after the heartbreaking Jayhawks tournament losses. There he was saying again and again that his players were good kids, that his players had character, that his players were hurting — and from the other side you certainly could take all that to mean that Kansas doesn't have kids as good, or players with as much character, and that losing hurts at North Carolina more than anywhere else.

You could take it that way, but I'd prefer not to. That's just Roy being Roy. He's an emotional guy. He gets carried away. He's also one heck of a basketball coach, and his teams play fun and thrilling basketball, and North Carolina will keep winning year after year for as long as Roy's there.

Then again, Kansas was going to the national-championship game. Kansas was the tougher team on Saturday. It was no accident: Bill Self coached them that way.

Joe Posnanski

2008 National Championship

April 7, 2008

Memphis Tigers

San Antonio, Texas

Kansas Coach Bill Self called a timeout late in the second half and gathered his team around him.

"This is the last time y'all are going to lace them up together," Self told the Jayhawks. "How do you want to leave on the court? Do you want to leave champions or do you want to leave losers?"

The Jayhawks had a resounding answer for Self: It would be as champions.

With two seconds left in regulation, Mario Chalmers put up an improbable three-pointer – and nailed it, tying the game. In the overtime after that, it was all Kansas. The Jayhawks scored the first six points and defeated Memphis for the NCAA championship.

They shocked the youthful and resilient Tigers and won the school's third NCAA title, its first since 1988 when Danny Manning and the Miracles upset Duke and Oklahoma in Kansas City.

"You couldn't have written it any better," said Russell Robinson, who as a senior was playing his last game for KU.

Twenty years ago, they won it with one man, Manning, taking a leading role. This year, they wore the crown thanks to a cast of characters that evolved over a five-month season into the definition of "team."

The greatest 20-year period in Kansas basketball history now had a bookend for its '88 title. That meant freedom from past demons. Good-bye, Arizona '97. See you later, Rhode Island '98. Nice knowing you, Bucknell and Bradley. The Jayhawks relieved themselves of any "choker" label and rewarded a diehard legion of fans.

Chalmers' game-tying three-pointer began the memory-erasing. Sayonara, Syracuse 2003.

All of it was forgotten when Chalmers' high, arching three swished to the roar of the crowd in San Antonio's Alamodome.

"He was born for moments such as this," said Chalmers' mother, Almarie.

Final score

Kansas....................................**75**

Memphis 68

A shot for the ages

Mario Chalmers sat on the podium in the moments after the game, and he wore his "National Champions" hat backward, he had a sort of dazed smile on his face, and he did not know. He could not know. He's history now.

"I was able to get a good look at it," he would say.

No, he did not know. He could not know. Chalmers made the shot. Kansas came back from nine down in the final furious seconds. Kansas beat Memphis 75-68 in overtime. The Jayhawks were national champions.

Kids 50 years hence would be shooting the Chalmers shot in driveways from Pittsburg to St. Francis, from Liberal to Hiawatha, from Cuba to Dodge City to Chanute. Grandparents in Wichita would call their grandchildren in Olathe to talk about what they were feeling when Chalmers took that shot, the way the ball arced, the way it fell. Farmers in Cuba and teachers in Salina and doctors in Garden City would talk about the shot forever.

There were precisely 43,257 fans in the Alamodome on Monday night to watch Kansas win its first championship in 20 years, but as time goes by there will be 100,000, then 200,000, then a million who will say they were here.

No, Mario Chalmers could not know because he's young. And when you're young, you live in the moment. That's how it's supposed to be. Chalmers was not feeling the pressure of history when he fired the shot. He never could have made it then. Kansas was trailing by nine points with barely 2 minutes left. Memphis had taken all the intensity and will and ferocity that Kansas had to give, and then the Tigers pulled away. Up nine with about 2 minutes left? Over.

"A lot of us thought the game was over," Kansas' Darnell Jackson would say.

"I thought we were national champs," Memphis coach John Calipari would say.

How did the comeback happen? It was a blur. A flurry. There was a huge steal by Kansas' gutsy Sherron Collins, followed by a three-pointer. There were some missed Memphis free throws. There were a couple of big shots by Kansas' Darrell Arthur.

Nobody could keep up with all the emotions of those final 10 seconds. Memphis' Derrick Rose had two free throws with the Tigers up two – if he made them both, then the Tigers would win. He missed the first. He made the second. Calipari told his players to foul so Kansas would not get a three-point

Mario Chalmers shouted in joy after making the three-point basket that tied the game in regulation. Facing page: Launching the clutch shot past Memphis defenders.

shot.

And Memphis' players tried to foul. They hammered Collins.

"I think I got fouled, actually," Collins said.

But there was no whistle. Collins managed to flip the basketball back to Chalmers. Memphis' incredible Rose was in his face.

"I was right there," Rose would say.

But Chalmers got the shot up. Reporters always ask, "What were you thinking?" when trying to relive moments like this one. And the answer never satisfies because to make a great play, you can't be thinking. Chalmers could not catch the ball and think about 20 years of frustration for Kansas basketball.

He could not think about the 1997 Kansas team, maybe the best in school history, and how those Jayhawks lost a heartbreaker to Arizona. He could not think about Nick Collison, one of the most complete players in the history of the school, who could not make his free throws in a championship game against Syracuse.

He could not think that Kansas – which belongs at the final table with the greatest basketball schools, with Kentucky, UCLA, North Carolina and Indiana – had won only one national championship in the last 56 years.

No, of course not. That's the beauty of youth. You don't think. You play. You live. Chalmers caught the pass, and he went up, and the ball felt great coming out of his hands. "I thought it was going in," he would say.

As we all watched the ball in the air, we knew it was history. We could tell.

As the ball swished through, everything in the game changed. Memphis' Chris Douglas-Roberts watched the rotation of the ball, and his head sagged. Bill Self, who had this crazy feeling, felt his heart beat in his chest.

The shot tied the game. But it really won the game. Memphis had no chance in overtime, not after that shot. When the game ended, when the confetti dropped, Memphis players walked slowly off the court. They knew that this loss would stay with them forever. The losing team always feels history first.

And the Jayhawks jumped around and cried and hugged.

"Are you aware of the historical significance of the shot you made tonight?" someone asked Chalmers.

"I mean," Mario would say with a smile, "it was a big shot for me."

Joe Posnanski

Danny's miracle deserved another

That's how you win it all, exorcise the demons and baptize a new era of greatness.

You do it with an unforgettable rally, a stunning three-pointer and with your most famous and infamous coaching alum sitting in the stadium, cheering you on and sporting a Jayhawk sticker

Dorothy said it best: "There's no place like (Kansas)," and now maybe Roy Williams and everybody else in the college basketball world realizes it, too.

Five years from heartbreak, feelings of betrayal and ruin, the Kansas Jayhawks became the kings of college basketball, winning their third NCAA title with a pulsating 75-68 overtime victory against the Memphis Tigers.

On the 20th anniversary of Danny Manning and the Miracles, Mario Chalmers' miracle three-pointer with 2.1 seconds left in regulation rescued the Jayhawks, culminated a furious 130-seconds rally from a nine-point hole and sent the championship spiraling into an extra session.

The Jayhawks were dead, down 60-51 with 2 minutes, 12 seconds to play and in desperate need of several miracles. They got a few along the way.

It really started when the refs correctly changed Memphis freshman Derrick Rose's apparent three-point basket to a two during a TV timeout with a little less than 4 minutes left in regulation.

That point would obviously prove to be critical. So would Memphis' three missed free throws in regulation's final 16 seconds. All season, basketball experts predicted the Tigers' free-throw-shooting woes would bite them.

When Chris Douglas-Roberts and Rose failed to extend Memphis' lead to two possessions by missing a combined three of four freebies, it cracked the door for Chalmers' heroics. When the Tigers failed to foul a Jayhawk and send Kansas to the line for two free throws, Memphis opened the door wide for a game-tying, miracle three-pointer.

Chalmers walked through that door, unspooling a floating rainbow from the top of the key.

It was good when it left his hand. It was great when it tickled the bottom of the net. And it became a permanent part

Twenty years after his team won KU's last national championship, Danny Manning embraced the 2008 squad on the night of its championship.

of Kansas history when the Jayhawks rode its momentum to a six-point advantage halfway through overtime.

"We got the ball into our most clutch player's hands, and he delivered," Kansas coach Bill Self said.

All of the Jayhawks delivered on this night.

Darrell Arthur scored 20 points and grabbed 10 rebounds. Brandon Rush dropped in 12 points and chased Douglas-Roberts all evening. Sherron Collins nailed a huge three late in regulation, passed out six assists and stole three balls. Darnell Jackson produced eight points and eight rebounds. Russell Robinson pestered Rose into a miserable first-half performance.

Chalmers did a little bit of everything, scoring 18, dishing out three assists and grabbing four steals. He was chosen the Final Four's Most Outstanding Player. He deserved it – on the big shot alone.

Self deserves some praise, too. He kept his team calm, confident and aggressive when it trailed by nine points and the game looked decided.

There will be a lot of talk about Memphis' collapse and John Calipari's coaching blunders.

"I take full responsibility," Calipari said in the aftermath. "When you're up seven (really nine) ... you're supposed to win that game. We were fouling late, and the kid got away from Derrick so he couldn't get to him to foul him, and

when he did get to him, knocked him to the floor and they just didn't call it. I understand why. And then they make a tough shot.

"Overtime, they kind of beat us down. I'm disappointed in myself. I look at that and say, 'We should have won that game.'"

Nope. Kansas was the better team. The Jayhawks controlled the entire first half and led by five at the break. The game got away from them for a stretch during the second half. But Kansas should've won in regulation.

Ed Hightower's officiating crew swallowed its whistle down the stretch. Collins got fouled hard going to the basket on a fast break late in the game. No call. Douglas-Roberts should've been called for a technical foul after he missed his two free throws late. He slammed the ball to the floor, sending the ball skyrocketing into the air. Hightower chose to talk to Douglas-Roberts rather than T him up.

The right team won this game. Once Collins' knee got healthy at the end of the regular season, the Jayhawks were the best team in college basketball. They proved it on Final Four weekend, demolishing a North Carolina team everyone thought was the best in the land and upending a Memphis team that had a chance to win a record number of games.

Kansas is king.

Jason Whitlock